SLC

The NO-NONSENSE GUIDE to
EQUALITY

'Publishers have created lists of short books that discuss the questions that your average [electoral] candidate will only ever touch if armed with a slogan and a soundbite. Together [such books] hint at a resurgence of the grand educational tradition... Closest to the hot headline issues are *The No-Nonsense Guides*. These target those topics that a large army of voters care about, but that politicos evade. Arguments, figures and documents combine to prove that good journalism is far too important to be left to (most) journalists.'

Boyd Tonkin,
The Independent,
London

D1300727

Dedication
To those who desire more.

About the author
Danny Dorling is a Professor of Human Geography at the University of Sheffield. With a group of colleagues, he helped create the website worldmapper.org which shows who has most and least in the world. He has co-written more than two dozen books on issues related to social inequalities as well as several hundred academic papers.

Acknowledgements
Chris Brazier suggested that this guide be written, encouraged me along the way and commented kindly and extensively on two drafts. Anna Barford, Noel Castree, Theresa Hayter, Bob Hughes, Sebastian Kraemer, Carl Lee, Brian Martin, Avner Offer, Chris Philo and Simon Reid-Henry all made comments on the initial suggestions as to what I should include and I am grateful to all of them. Tom Mills suggested the C Wright Mills quotation at the start of Chapter 6. David Gordon and Nigel Waters both made comments used towards the end of Chapter 4. Richard Wilkinson and Kate Pickett advised on both an early and a late draft. Alison, Bronwen and David Dorling all helped iron out the English, argument and structure. Chris Brazier then ironed it again, all to save you time and confusion in reading. It takes a lot of work by many people to make even something this small. Thanks!

About the New Internationalist
New Internationalist is an independent, not-for-profit publishing co-operative that reports on issues of global justice. We publish informative current affairs and popular reference titles, complemented by multicultural recipe books, photography and fiction from the Global South, as well as calendars, diaries and cards – all with a global justice world view.

If you like this *No-Nonsense Guide* you will also enjoy the *New Internationalist* magazine. The freshly designed magazine is packed full of quality writing, in-depth analysis and new features, including:
- Agenda: cutting-edge reports
- Argument: heated debate between experts
- Analysis: understanding the key global issues
- Action: making change happen
- Alternative living: inspiring ideas
- Arts: the best of global culture.

To find out more about the **New Internationalist**, visit our website at **www.newint.org**

The  NO-NONSENSE GUIDE to

EQUALITY

Danny Dorling

NewInternationalist

The No-Nonsense Guide to Equality
Published in the UK in 2012 by New Internationalist™ Publications Ltd
55 Rectory Road
Oxford OX4 1BW, UK
www.newint.org
New Internationalist is a registered trade mark.

Cover image: Tao/Robert Harding

Series editor: Chris Brazier
Design by New Internationalist Publications Ltd.

Printed in UK by Bell and Bain Ltd.
who hold environmental accreditation ISO 14001.

MIX
Paper from
responsible sources
FSC® C007785

British Library Cataloguing-in-Publication Data.
A catalogue record for this book is available from the British Library.

Library of Congress Cataloguing-in-Publication Data.
A catalogue for this book is available from the Library of Congress.

ISBN 978-1-78026-071-6

Foreword

DANNY DORLING's *No-Nonsense Guide to Equality* needs reading twice. In a world where so much that doesn't matter is slickly promoted in day-glo colors to grab unwarranted attention, Danny makes important points thick and fast, with so little build-up that you can easily miss them. He gets to the core of greater equality by asking – as if in passing – 'What use would your wealth be if others did not need wages to be your servants?' We often fail to recognize how inextricably wealth and poverty are bound together. The presence of wealthy people creates a sense of relative deprivation and the need for higher wages among the less well-off. As Danny says, 'what is enough depends on how much more those above you have.'

The social anthropologist Marshall Sahlins said of people in early hunting and gathering societies: '[they] have few possessions, but they are not poor.' He then went on to say: 'Poverty is not a certain small amount of goods, nor is it just a relation between means and ends; above all it is a relation between people. Poverty is a social status. As such, it is an invention of civilization. It has grown with civilization... as an invidious distinction between classes...'[1]

An important issue facing the modern world is the way economic growth serves as a sop for the dissatisfactions and social tensions which result from great inequality. Henry Wallich, a former governor of the US Federal Reserve and professor of economics at Yale University, put it like this: 'Growth is a substitute for equality of income. So long as there is growth there is hope, and that makes large income differentials tolerable.'[2] By 'hope', Wallich meant that rising material standards over time produced a sense of self-advancement – of moving up – that might serve as a substitute for the sense of self-advancement produced by moving up the social ladder.

However, economic growth is now severely curtailed by the international financial turmoil since the crash of 2008 and, even without that, would need to be reined in to reduce carbon emissions. (We should distinguish here between the growth of resource use, which the rich countries need to avoid, and the technical and social innovation needed to bring us towards sustainability.)

So what if growth can no longer substitute for equality? When growth halted in the Great Depression of the 1930s, there were very rapid reductions in inequality. The motive for policies which contributed to the decline in inequality almost certainly included a desire to reduce what was then the growing support for socialism and communism: the Depression was, after all, regarded by many as the long-heralded collapse of capitalism that socialists had predicted.

Now that the threat of communism has largely passed, there may be less pressure on politicians to reduce inequality as a way of maintaining political support. Nevertheless, the signs are that the public tolerance for astronomical top salaries and bonuses, for tax avoidance among both wealthy individuals and companies, is rapidly disappearing. No-one believes there is anything 'fair' about paying for the mistakes of bankers and hedge-fund executives (especially while they continue to receive grossly inflated incomes) by cutting public services, which are used predominantly by the least well-off and most vulnerable.

If economic growth is less forthcoming, whether because of the long-term effects of the financial crash or as a result of the need to reduce carbon emissions, the pressure for greater equality is likely to increase. There is another important link between environmental issues and greater equality. Consumerism is almost certainly the greatest threat to reducing carbon emissions. The reduction of inequality is a necessary first step to achieving sustainability because consumerism is driven by status competition which – in turn – is intensified by having less equality.

Lastly, as we showed in our book *The Spirit Level*, greater equality seems to improve the real quality of life for the vast majority of the population.[3] It improves the quality of social relations and dramatically reduces the scale of health and social problems in societies. Indeed, the data suggest that, to make further improvements in the real quality of our lives, we need to shift our attention from material standards as driven by consumerism to improving the quality of social relations. What is exciting is that the evidence suggests we can achieve this by reducing the material differences between us.

Looking only at the effects of income differences, in our research we took a very simple view of inequality. What is refreshing about Danny's *No-Nonsense Guide to Equality* is how multi-faceted and rich in insights it is. That makes it an important contribution to creating a wider understanding of inequality.

Richard Wilkinson, Emeritus Professor, University of Nottingham, and *Kate Pickett*, Professor, University of York.

1 Marshal Sahlins, *Stone Age Economics*, Tavistock, London, 1974. 2 Henry C Wallich, 'Zero Growth', *Newsweek*, 24 Jan 1972. 3 Richard Wilkinson and Kate Pickett, *The Spirit Level: why equality is better for everyone*, Penguin 2009.

CONTENTS

Introduction

WHEN I SAID I was trying to write a guide to equality, what was most interesting about the comments I received was how varied was the advice that was offered. Hardly anyone studies equality.[1] Huge numbers of people are concerned with inequality. Almost all of these people lament the extent to which inequalities have grown, but there appears to be little shared ground over the benefits of a more equal city, country and world.

It is as if so many of us have been moving away from greater equality for so many years that it is now considered fanciful to ask how we might live better. However, without an idea of where it is you want to get to, constantly opposing where you are heading can become exhausting. The most common route to greater equality is simply ensuring that next year is a little less unfair than this year, and doing that repeatedly, sometimes for longer than a human lifetime.

I usually precede 'equality' with the word 'greater' because this guide is more about a direction than a destination. I provide numerous examples of how just moving in that direction increases the well-being and happiness of the vast majority, but subverts the wishes of those who believe you can never have too much, a group who can never be satisfied.

This book is a very personal view of greater equality, its benefits and what are seen as the possible downsides of us all becoming more equal. It takes an optimistic stance because it is very easy to become pessimistic when considering inequalities. The tendency is to concentrate all the time on the current worst excesses of inequality and then to extrapolate from that point.

In medical science there is always a disease that is becoming more common. In affluent countries it was cholera, then tuberculosis, then heart disease, then cancers, now dementia. In poorer countries it was diarrhea and then AIDS and now malaria (again). Medics are largely concerned with ill-health, not with good health, and to someone who sees ill people every day, illness is all around. But most of us in the world have seen huge improvements in our overall health, largely due to better sanitation, nutrition and public health, but also through medical advances, including vaccination. Most of us have also benefited from periods of rising equality.

The vast majority of people in the world enjoy greater equality in so many more ways than did their great-grandparents. In relation to men, the position of women has improved most markedly. As mortality during childbirth continues to decline, for the first time in human history, women – any day now – are about to make up a majority of humans on the planet. Another example of progress is that few people now live in colonies (as explicitly defined). Fewer people are governed by obvious dictators than ever before.

Only recently have a majority of children worldwide been treated as being equal enough in value to other children to be taught to read and write – and, again, this is the first time in human history this has happened.

At the same time, most people are enjoying less equality in many ways within their country than their parents did. Women make up the large majority of the world's poor. Death in childbirth remains the biggest killer of women. More of us now, worldwide, live at the whims of colonizing corporate organizations, some of whose employees suggest that there is no alternative to concentrating primarily on inhuman profit-taking. For the first time in history, we could easily prevent the majority of the millions of deaths that are suffered by very young children every year, but we choose not to. At least we now have the choice.

The technologies and knowledge that gave us this choice were only developed themselves in places where enough equalities had been won to allow more than the élite to join in the study of medicine and science, and

Introduction

so make the advances. If greater equality has been, and continues to be, the underlying solution to so much that troubles people, then it is worth concentrating for once on what you gain from it, not on what you suffer as a result of inequality. This *No-Nonsense Guide* explains what is good about having more equality, and offers a few thoughts on how greater equality is won.

Danny Dorling
Sheffield, November 2011

1 For those that do, see Utopian Studies Society: utopianstudieseurope.org and Ruth Levitas's 2005 Inaugural Lecture 'The Imaginary Reconstitution of Society: or why sociologists and others should take Utopia seriously'. Available here: bris.ac.uk/spais/files/inaugural.pdf

1 Why equality matters

In a world that often lionizes wealth, it is worth remembering that no-one can be rich unless others are poor. In the world's more equal countries, more infants survive and people are generally healthier and happier. Equality pays dividends at every stage of human life, from babyhood to old age.

'There's ultimately a very small number of people that are phenomenally bright but also have the skills to run a company, the social skills to run a company at that level. It's just the nature of the world ... If this person has those skills, then he deserves the money.'
Male, 37, private sector, earning
more than £100,000 ($160,000) a year[1]

EQUALITY MATTERS because, when you have less of it, you have to put up with obnoxious behavior, insulting suggestions and stupid ideas such as the one above, that it is the 'nature of the world' that 'a very small number of people' are 'phenomenally bright'.

Equality matters because human beings are creatures that thrive in societies where we are treated more as equals than as being greatly unequal in mental ability, sociability or any other kind of ability. We work best, behave best, play best and think best when we are not laboring under the assumption that some of us are much better, more deserving and so much more able than others. We perform the worst, are most atrocious in our conduct, are least relaxed and most unimaginative in outlook, when we live under the weight of great inequalities – and especially under the illusion that these are somehow warranted.

Inequalities harm the rich as well as the poor. The rich are not necessarily especially hard working, well behaved, happy or creative. Some are obsessed with making money and can be driven by that. Most behave much better when they are more like the rest of us. They can have appalling social skills while believing that they are 'phenomenally bright'. Many don't understand that it is questionable why the poor should work hard for a pittance, obey the law, or any other conventions, when the poor are members of a group being treated so unfairly.

How can people have the time and energy to contribute to our overall understanding and enjoyment of life when they are thinking of the world under delusions either of superiority or of inferiority? Inequality matters because it brings out the worst in us all. An actor called Mae West spent a lifetime accidentally explaining this. She became famous, which is why we are starting with her.

In times of great inequality, we are fooled into thinking of celebrity as greatness. This is why Hollywood celebrities were so lauded in the 1920s and why they are again today, especially in those countries where inequalities had, before, grown greatest, such as around Hollywood itself in the 1920s, and in most of the United States again now.

The Zen of Mae West

All too often, when greater equality is advocated, the words of Mae West – a woman born plain Mary Jane – are quoted as if her particular wisdom were of special value because of her celebrity. Mary Jane chose the name Mae to use on stage. It was popular at the time. These are her famous words that are so often still repeated in one form or another when discussing the merits of greater equality: *'I've been rich and I've been poor. Believe me, rich is better.'*

Greater equality would mean a few people not being quite so rich, and for many of them, that means (relatively speaking, in their perception) being poor. Because of this, some suggest that it is better not to have too much equality. The suggestion is that it is far better to be rich if you can, and to get out of poverty by aiming to be rich too. This is seen as preferable to the idea that everyone would benefit from being a little more equal. The dozen words in the quotation above play on the notion that the poor will always be with us, so the only sensible aim in life is to avoid being among them. Mae suggests that the best way to avoid poverty is to become rich.

Mae West was born in 1892 and died in 1980. She lived through a fortunate time. She got to see a great deal of poverty eliminated and inequalities greatly decline through most of her adult years. But she appeared not to appreciate it that much. She was born in Brooklyn, New York, in the United States of America. She became a movie star. Her upbringing was not particularly poor and she didn't experience much poverty later in life. In fact, her family had been wealthy enough to purchase a series of five crypts in 1930 in a prestigious New York cemetery, one of which she would eventually be buried in. It is certainly true that Mae had been rich, but there is less evidence of her experiencing much poverty.

Offered a choice between poverty and riches, most people would choose the latter. Another of Mae's famous quotations reads: '*When choosing between two evils, I always like to try the one I've never tried before.*' She was being funny and she was not necessarily comparing riches and poverty, but inequality and evil are not that funny. Poverty and riches are both evils. It is not possible to be rich without others being poor and few people would advocate increasing poverty.

Being rich is having more than others. Getting richer is getting even more than others; by definition, getting richer is at others' expense. But there is no need to choose between evils. You can choose to be more equal, you can choose for there to be both less riches and less poverty, you can choose the right thing, you can choose that you want to be more like others in what your money allows you to do, in how much you have.

But isn't it possible for all of us to become richer, or at least for a great many people to gain wealth? Isn't that what occurred between plain Mary Jane's Brooklyn childhood and Mae West's Los Angeles death? Didn't the standard of living of almost all Americans rise greatly? It did, but that is not the same as all Americans becoming rich. Mae confused a better living standard with greater riches. It is a common mistake to make. In fact, living standards for all rise significantly *only* when the continuing growth in the riches of a few very wealthy people has been curtailed.

Being rich means having much wealth. Wealth means having an abundance of possessions and, as the *Oxford English Dictionary* puts it: an abundance 'especially of money'. Money is a medium of exchange; it is used to buy things: commodities, land, labor. 'Abundance' is: *'a very great quantity, especially more than enough'*. Being rich is about having more than others and more than you need. That might be better than being poor, but if you have more than you *need* – of the means of exchange (money) – others have to have less than they need. If they did not have less than they needed you would not be rich.

You can have more than you need of love, of learning, of friendship, of warmth. People will rarely accuse you of being too gentle a person, too nice, too trustworthy or truthful. You can simultaneously have enough personal material possessions to keep you in comfort. But you cannot have more of the means of exchange than you need without also automatically having the right to call on the time, labor and property of others. That is what an abundance of riches gives you – the ability to curtail the freedoms of others, to be able to make choices which curtail their choices.

What, then, is enough? I once commented about how many shoes a friend of mine had in his family's hallway. He replied (a few months later, he'd been thinking about it) that he thought his family had fewer shoes than many in the UK, and that he had survived a year in India on a pair of flip-flops and a pair of trainers which was enough, but not enough when appearances mattered. What is 'enough' in affluent societies is most often decided in comparison with what others have and expect, and it tends to be more, the greater inequality there is.

If you were rich you might not worry about others having less than they need, fewer possessions than are essential for their respectability, or worry about others having less choice, less freedom than you. You might think it necessary. After all, how could you purchase the labor of others (to do the work you might not want to do) if they did not have less than they needed?

What use would your riches be if others did not need wages to be your servants? Would you just buy more and more possessions and then dust them yourself? Some people never see others as like themselves. Mae herself said *'I never loved another person the way I loved myself'*. Mae had no children. She may never have loved another person much, but she may also not have loved herself that much – despite being so rich.

Living standards are not about having more than enough. Going back to the dictionary and looking up definitions often helps us see straight. A standard is a measure of *quality* often recognized as a *model for imitation*. A living is a means of maintenance, a livelihood. Living standards are those means of maintaining ourselves which are of a certain quality and which can and should be replicated widely (a model for imitation).

Living standards are about having *enough*. But the problem is that what is enough depends on how much more those above you have. If they have closets full of shoes, then your five pairs per family member may appear meager (boots, trainers, smart shoes, deck shoes, flip flops[2]). Well, maybe it's time to give Mae some credit for some of what she said. After all, she said a lot of things and they cannot all have been bunkum. According to Mae, once is enough: *'You only live once, but if you do it right, once is enough.'*

Having enough is having what is right in the circumstances you find you are living in. What was enough in 1890s Brooklyn would have been far too little to exist on in 1980s Los Angeles. Even though most of the worse-off people in 1980s Los Angeles, where Mae died, were each on average unbelievably more prosperous than were the residents of that (still being built) Brooklyn borough in New York almost a century earlier. But that did not mean that the living standards of the poor in Los Angeles were high – because humans are social animals. Living standards have always been measured in contemporary comparison to others, since only by comparison can we assess quality.

By the 1980s it had become common to own a car in Los Angeles. It was one of the first cities in the world where car ownership became a norm. To be poor in Los Angeles then was not to own a car. Just over 80 years earlier, when Mary Jane was a child in Brooklyn, only the very richest people owned a car; no factory lines to mass produce cars existed. You didn't *need* a car in 1900s Brooklyn, no matter who you were. By the 1980s, and across that continent, it became almost impossible to be part of society without a car. In the United States today many homeless people sleep in their cars.

Winning greater equality for babies

Babies are great levelers because they are all more or less the same – and also the same as they were 10,000 years ago. So let's begin with babies.

One way to see why greater equality matters to people is to look across a human lifetime. As Mae said, you've got to live it right, you'll only have one. At each age you can consider whether people in general are better-off when their living conditions are more equal, or whether living in a family that has great riches might be better for an individual than being more average. It is also worth considering if there are any ages at which living in poverty is more or less harmful than at other ages.

One way in which campaigners for greater equality succeed is by striving to reduce poverty. Demanding that child poverty be abolished is a particularly good tactic because few people argue that any child deserves to be poor. Sadly, however, there are people who try to divide the poor into those who they suggest are deserving of some aid and those who are supposedly undeserving. These same people often then suggest that nobody should have a child if they cannot afford to. They rarely ask why (in some very rich countries today) many people feel they cannot afford to become parents.

The first age of life (following William Shakespeare's famous 'seven ages' speech from *As You Like It*) is infanthood – from birth until school. Greater equality has some very clear benefits to infants. In affluent societies with more equitable income distributions, fewer babies are born undernourished. They also suffer less from diseases caused by the alcohol or drugs taken by their mothers while they were in the womb. This is because use of alcohol and drugs is less prevalent amongst adults in more equitable societies.[3]

In poorer societies, infants are more likely to die within their first year of life than in richer societies, but in more equitable poor societies those risks are also reduced. In the year 2009, worldwide, 42 babies died for every 1,000 born. However, in Cuba infant mortality rates were 10 times less at 4 per 1,000, even less than in the hugely wealthier United States of America (7 per 1,000). In very unequal and poor

Why equality matters

India, the rate was 50 deaths per 1,000 born and in more equitable and a little less poor China it was 17 per 1,000. For every grieving parent in China each day there were three in India.[4] Where would you rather have a child if you were an average citizen? Remember there is also childhood mortality and illness to consider, not just surviving the first year.

You could say it is better to give birth in a rich country than in any poor country today, and in terms of child survival this usually is true.[5] However, again you must choose carefully. The rates of infant deaths per 1,000 live births in Iceland and Japan, which currently stand at 2, are less than a third of those in the US.[6] Iceland and Japan are the most equitable of affluent countries and these infant mortality rates suggest that two-thirds of all the infants who die every year in the US are dying because of the great levels of inequalities tolerated in that country and the social ills associated with those inequalities.

Iceland and Japan have suffered great economic hardship in recent years, yet their more equitable societies are better placed to absorb the effects of this – the average family in these two countries is far better off, by many ways of measuring quality of life, than the average family in the more unequal affluent nations. However, in most countries, quality of life is now much better than it was in the recent past. This is also down to equality and especially to the greater equalities that were won almost everywhere not too long ago; in the United States, as well as in very different Iceland, as well as half a world away in India.

Just over a century ago Britain was the richest country in the world. Nevertheless, the infant mortality rates suffered by the newborn children of the very richest people in Britain stood at around 100 per 1,000 babies born. These were the people with high enough incomes to be able to pay servants to cook and clean for them. Now, only nine of the very poorest countries of the world still suffer rates as high as that. In many ways it is better to be born poor now than to have been born rich a century ago, but this is only because so much progress has been made.

No affluent group anywhere in the world now suffers anything comparable to the rates of infant death that the children of the British aristocracy suffered a century ago. In Britain early on, and in many less affluent countries a little later, rates of infectious diseases (those diseases which still kill most infants globally) had been brought down enormously by immunization and better sanitation. It was the introduction of better sanitation for all in Britain, most importantly the introduction of sewers, which did most to protect the children of the rich (as well as the poor). It was greater equality. Sewers make us all more equal. They are a public good.

Usually it is the struggle of poorer groups that results in greater equality being won. People go on strike to have poverty wages raised. They very occasionally, but with great effect, overturn despotic rulers in revolutions. When revolutions are orchestrated by any group other than the élite, as occurred in France, the United States, Russia, China and Cuba, the results are always greater equality. Often much bloodshed and new forms of tyranny follow and inequalities can rise again, though rarely to their previous heights. The new forms of tyranny often result from increasing internal security in response to outside threats. It is perhaps only in the United States that inequalities today are higher than they were before its revolution (often called its war of independence).

Greater equality is occasionally demanded by the rich. For the rich, the benefits are less obvious and because the rich hold so much power they tend usually to act as a brake upon greater equalities being won. Yet in Britain at the start of the 20th century it became obvious to many rich people that greater equality was in their interest, too – the rich were among those agitating for the great public works that were undertaken to improve social goods such as sanitation. A few of the rich also argued for pensions for all, for unemployment benefit and for child allowances. Some of the rich today are still not as blinkered as most of them unfortunately remain.

Of sewers and cathedrals

If you look around the world today, into the megacities especially, you can see great public works being undertaken almost everywhere. Because sewers run underground they are not as visible as are the great mosques, palaces, temples and cathedrals of the world and yet, in the last few decades, we have built underground more cubic meters of sewer and storm drain worldwide than all the volume of the world's majestic public buildings ever constructed above ground. And whereas only a select few are allowed in each palace, the sewers are for everyone's waste.

Our eyes are more often drawn to new slums, and not to where former slums are turning into poor but permanent neighborhoods. Rulers sanction the building of sewers, of these cathedrals below ground, because they are as much in their personal interest as in their subjects' interest; but rulers are quicker to do this where the gap between them and those they rule is narrower.

Often huge numbers of poor people are unfairly evicted from areas which are being gentrified. Slum clearance is rarely a fair form of progress. The poor frequently turn out not to have legal rights, which is another source of great inequality. But in aggregate the global infant mortality rate continues to fall. By April 2011 it was reported, for 2009, to be 42 children per 1,000 born. It was twice that in 1975.

The absolute fall in the number of grieving parents has been even greater than the fall in the worldwide infant mortality rate. Between the years 1970-74 and

2005-09 world population increased by 67 per cent, but the number of children the average woman in the world was giving birth to (in her lifetime) fell from 4.45 to 2.52 babies, or by 43 per cent. Combining the falls in fertility and rise in population, this is some 28 per cent fewer babies being born.[7] So, in absolute terms, there are much less than half the number of grieving parents in the world now than there were in the early 1970s, even though world population is now much larger. That is real progress.

There is one exception to the general rule that, among affluent countries, infant mortality rates are lowest in those nations that are more equitable. That exception is Singapore which, according to the UN, has a very low rate of two babies dying per thousand born alive in 2009. How then does Singapore manage to maintain very high income inequalities – the highest amongst the 26 richest nations of the world[8] – but also have one of the lowest infant mortality rates?

Some of the poorest people in Singapore are the maids, who are servants for one in five of all middle-class households. The maids act as personal cleaners, shoppers and child-carers. Most of the maids are guest-workers from abroad. They have no right to remain in Singapore. In more economically unequal countries the poor tend to have fewer legal rights. Every six months they must take a pregnancy test and, if they are found to be pregnant, they are deported.

Migrant workers make up about a quarter of the population of Singapore and are mainly at the bottom of the income range, where you'd expect infant mortality to be highest. This section of the population is effectively removed from the picture by deportation and the threat of it. Poorer women trying very hard not to become pregnant is one way in which infant mortality can be reduced. The babies who would have a greater chance of dying are never actually born.

The reason infant mortality rates in Singapore are

lower than in almost all European countries is not the good public health levels, which are similar to the better standards in Europe, but the deportation threat for 'guest-workers', which is not widely replicated in Europe.

It is obvious that your mother losing her job and being sent somewhere with worse medical facilities to have her baby in is clearly detrimental to the unborn children of many of the poor in Singapore. But does the deportation of maids who become pregnant also harm the infant children of the rich in Singapore, those they are often paid to care for? Is Singapore a model that rich people around the world could try to emulate if they did not care about the servants? Can the rich in future shield themselves from the lives of the poor by evicting poor people when their presence no longer suits?

In some ways the nation-state of Singapore is a country that acts like a very large Victorian British country house. In these country houses, servants were expelled if found pregnant. Aristocrats didn't want servants' children cluttering up the place and servants could not afford to pay others to care for their children. So naturally, if a maid became pregnant she had to leave. There was, of course, nothing natural about this (which is why, in Britain today, the idea of working 'in service' is still so resented).

However, just because gross inequalities within a country like Britain became (for a long time) untenable does not mean such inequalities cannot be maintained across state borders. Many maids in Singapore do have children but return to work, leaving their child with its grandmother or another relative. The money they send home ensures the survival of both. But is this a sensible way of living for the rich as well as the poor?

Where inequalities are great and poverty is widespread, the short-term incentive grows ever greater for the rich to segregate and cut themselves off in great country estates or smaller gated communities. In India, most of the rich work hard to insulate themselves from the poor – they want not to see them, often not even to acknowledge their existence. Wine bars in Mumbai skyscrapers are so high up that people on the streets below appear smaller than ants. But those ants will be the sisters, fathers and children of the servants of the rich.

From the spread of infectious diseases that feed on poverty, to the fear of armed insurrection one day occurring, maintaining high levels of inequality within a country for decades is both very damaging to wider public health and well-being, and very hard to achieve politically.

One way to begin to answer the question as to whether the perpetuation of inequalities in a place like Singapore is sensible is to ask if it also harms the rich. Think whether you would be better off being brought up by a servant with no lifetime commitment to you, or by your parents. Think whether you would rather sort out your own food to eat, or always have it presented to you. It is rumored that the heir to the throne in Britain has a servant who dresses him each day. But wouldn't you rather pull up your own trousers? Once you become reliant on servants for parts of your life, it is easy to become less capable of doing those things yourself.

Being brought up by a woman who is all the time thinking of the child she has had to leave behind is not something to be envied. The Victorian English rich were not a joyous bunch. They were an historical aberration. The citadel of Singapore, sitting at the crossroads of world cargo-ship trade, has boomed in recent years only because so many trinkets are now made in China and transported so far by sea using so much oil. Some 900 years ago, the city of Merv on the silk route was claimed to be the largest in the world. Its ancient ruins are a world heritage site and yet you almost certainly have not heard of it.[9] It came and it went.

The worst effects of inequality for children

Equality matters hugely to children. Most children are brought up almost entirely within a loving family until they are old enough to go to school, and after that still spend more of their waking hours in their family. Families tend to be models of equality and co-operation.[10] They are usually far from perfect, and some are very brutal. Nevertheless, it is increasingly common that financial resources are shared equitably within a family, that parents try to treat all their children as equals, and that children are brought up to consider their parents as people they will treat as equals in future, not as their betters or elders.

Most families are made up of a man and a woman and, unlike many of their parents and most of their grandparents, these men and women increasingly try to treat each other as equals and are expected by others to do so. In a variety of religions all over the world, and almost always when bound together in secular ceremonies, far fewer women than in the past promise to 'obey' their husbands when they marry.[11] Unprecedented numbers of couples feel no compulsion to go through formal marriage ceremonies at all, but almost all couples understand the need to be loving parents.

A few children are not brought up in loving families. In the past, in what are now affluent countries, many infants had to be abandoned by their parents because they could not afford to care for them and also feed themselves. If left as babies to be discovered, these were called foundlings, and orphanages were built to care for them as one of the earliest signs of greater equality being won. Before then, such babies were left to die, or smothered shortly after birth.

Many children in the poorest and least equitable

countries in the world still have to be abandoned because of destitution. In some (rare) cases, infanticide (more often of baby girls than boys) is still practiced because of extreme poverty. Even in the most unequal rich countries, some children are still given up by their parents because they find they cannot care for them. Most are given up for adoption, but there are still a couple of 'foundling' children registered every year in countries like the UK.[12]

Far more teenagers become parents in the most unequal of affluent countries, and it is these teenagers who are most likely to give up their children. Children are also more likely to live with just one of their parents in more unequal countries – marriages tend to break up more often given the economic and social strains of living in a more unequal society.[13]

At the extreme of global society, in affluent but unequal countries, the children of the very rich can often have very little contact with their parents. This is usually not because their parents are callous; almost all parents want to spend time with their children and get to know them. All children want more time with loving parents and carers.

The reasons why very affluent adults often spend too little time with their offspring include social convention, where the servants are there to 'see to' the children, and family traditions of sending sons or daughters to boarding school. Other affluent parents often feel they need to work long hours to maintain their privileged position in an unequal society.

It was social conventions that led to those English servant-keeping classes a century ago suggesting that children should be seen and not heard. Conventionally, children would be brought down by nanny and presented in a row for the adults to inspect before they (the adults) started their evening meal.

The children of the rich ate with nanny in the nursery. Their real parent was the nanny but, sadly, the nannies were often changed. This was akin to losing your parents over and over again.[14] Although this was clearly nothing like as harmful as actually being orphaned, very little attention is paid to how much the children of the very rich suffered in the past from the conventions that went with extreme affluence. Hardly anyone today talks of the emotional problems of contemporary rich children. It might be good if we did.

Children brought up in institutions, child prisons, boarding schools, care homes and the like rarely talk of the experiences they had with much happiness.[15] They are often very bitter about the choices the adults in their early lives made over their care. These experiences also appear to extend even to institutions established to bring up children in a spirit of greater equality – kibbutzim and communes.

Sometimes children brought up outside of families become convinced that some aspects of their treatment hardened them, or better prepared them for a harsh world. But what they usually say is that the institutions are much better now than then. This might be true – but as I've grown older I've noticed the next generation of incumbents say much the same thing.

In more equitable countries, far fewer children, both rich and poor, are separated from their parents due to long work hours, to being sent away from home to study, to being taken into care or to being imprisoned. In some of the most equitable Scandinavian countries I have been told that the government minister responsible for imprisonment knows personally the handful of children who are incarcerated. They are so few that she or he can remember their names.

In an equitable society, all children are different, but in some ways they are more similar than in unequal nations. Hardly any are hungry, for instance. The consumption of toys and other goods in more equitable nations tends to be lower. Less has to be transported from China. Far less money is spent on advertising in such countries and less of that advertising is aimed at making children feel inferior and encouraging them to pester their parents. Such advertising directed at children is more likely to be banned.[16]

Where children grow up in similar economic circumstances to other children around them, they have less need to show off. Children are more likely to play together if they do not live in gated compounds in cities without sidewalks (such compounds are common now in more unequal affluent places). They are more likely to have child-centered childhoods, whereas affluent children in affluent countries now spend far more time with adults, often being coached to compete educationally in out-of-hours teaching sessions or sitting in the car talking to mother (not mum or ma) while being driven to some apparently socially appropriate activity, rather than playing freely with the local kids.

Everyone knows, or should know, that the poor do much worse in more unequal societies – they are simply poorer. What far too few people know is that the children of the rich also fare worse under such conditions – not just from the anxiety and depression they are more likely to suffer,[17] but also from the growing sense that they have been denied a normal childhood with lots of play.

The benefits of equality in childhood

Children are very sensitive to inequality. It has been suggested by a great many researchers that human beings are essentially programmed to be incredibly aware of slights and unfairness.[18] The whine of 'that's not fair' is dreaded by parents because it requires a far more complicated and considered response than is needed to react appropriately to: 'I want it – give me'. At home, within the household, there are often pecking orders. Older siblings will usually dominate younger siblings, but they might also be required to care for them and assist them. Men often dominate women; in many places such domination is now less frequent as greater equality between the sexes is being won. Gender and age hierarchies still exist, but much less almost everywhere than was the case just a generation ago.

Families in which greater inequality and unfairness are tolerated tend not to be very happy. At one extreme of domestic inequality, a child grows up watching one parent abuse another. In more equitable societies, all forms of domestic abuse (physical, sexual, emotional and economic) are far less common, including the fairly easily counted rate of child murder.

Some historians claim that, until recently, childhood in much of the world was a very short-lived and often quite brutal experience; they claim that it has only been in very recent times and only under conditions of much greater equality that child labor has not been required and that children have been both seen and heard within families. But this was apparently the case a long time ago too. The offspring of hunter-gatherers do not become net providers until the age of 20.[19] We evolved to have a long childhood of learning and playing.

All over the world it has become widely unacceptable to hit children; their views have to be taken into account and their happiness cherished. Bullying, which was common in the very recent past, and even encouraged so as to 'harden up' children, has suddenly become recognized as something to be ashamed of. Corporal punishment is now outlawed in many countries. It was still common 30 years ago.

It is when children go to school that they often discover stark inequalities for the first time. In more equitable countries, children are more likely to attend their nearest school. This reduces the amount of time and money children and their parents need to waste commuting to school (and reduces traffic congestion).

Going to school locally also means that their school friends can easily live next door or nearby, which reduces the strange new fashion in unequal countries for affluent children to be transported in cars to 'play-dates' arranged by their parents. In more equitable countries, 20-mile-per-hour or 30-kilometer-per-hour speed limits are more common on residential roads and parents are happier to let their children cross such roads alone, freeing up the time of women in particular. Local speed limits are now just beginning to be seen as an issue associated with improving gender equality.

In countries where people live more similar lives to each other, children tend to be less closely monitored and controlled. Often, formal schooling starts later in life, when a child is aged six rather than four. Examination and ranking of children tends to be less frequent in more equitable societies where there is less apparent need to begin to sort children into different roles early on. And children are usually safer. Child mortality rates are lower where economic equality is higher.

In more equal societies and during more equitable times, children get to mix with a wider variety of other children and so tend to gain a better grasp of their society as a whole.[20] In more unequal societies, places within private schools are reserved only for the few who can afford to pay very high fees. These schools help segregate the children of the rich from other children.

One of the worse effects of private schooling is that it can imbue an unhealthy sense of superiority among those affluent children who have been deprived of the opportunity to mix with others. Often they receive high examination marks, which is hardly surprising, as that is mostly what their parents have paid for. It is easy to confuse jumping well through these hoops (like well-trained puppies) with proof of superior intelligence. They think of their private schools as a better education, but if it teaches them to look down on other people, it cannot be.

Why equality matters

When a greater proportion of children are educated together, rather than segregated by either their parents' wealth or their supposed ability, by parents' faith or by child's sex (or both), all the children on aggregate have a better experience of education and emerge as more knowledgeable, caring and imaginative. Boys and girls, if separated into different schools on the basis of gender, have knowledge of roughly half the population denied them. Reducing segregation is beneficial to all; even the crudest of examination results reveal this, but I'll just give you one anecdote.

I used to live in Bristol, one of England's more affluent larger cities. Bristol at the time suffered very little unemployment, its housing was expensive and incomes tended to be higher than average, and yet from Bristol proportionately fewer children found their way to study at university than from the large city I now live in, which is Sheffield. Sheffield has for decades suffered higher unemployment than Bristol, its housing is much cheaper and a great deal of it was built by local government; incomes are on average much lower, and it is also a divided city by wealth. So why do more children from Sheffield get to university than from Bristol?

The simple answer is that Sheffield has very few private schools, whereas Bristol has many. The children from Bristol whose parents pay for them to attend private school often get higher exam results, and most of them go to university. But the overall effect of taking these children out of the general state system is to reduce the funding for that system (which is per child) and to convince many children that they need to go to a non-state school to have a chance to get to university.

In contrast, in Sheffield, children from similar backgrounds to Bristol's privately educated children are in state schools and so for all children in those schools the sense that they are worthy of further education is raised. For the city as a whole, it is cheaper and more effective not to segregate children. Sheffield may not be segregated by much of a state/private education divide but it is still divided geographically into areas with state secondary education that tends to lead on to university, and areas where it doesn't. Nevertheless, more children proportionately get to university from the poorer city. If Bristol had as much state education it would be fair to assume that even more children from there would go (given that it is a richer city overall).

So why do parents waste their money on private education? One reason is that they have the money to waste. In more equitable societies, there are fewer rich parents who can afford to pay for their children not to have to sit near others at school. However, another reason is that no-one is employed to explain the downsides. Not just the aggregate downsides, which they may well not care about, or the fact that their child might do just as well, if not better, in the state system (which no-one is paid to tell them about), but also that they might be reducing their offspring's future options. Growing up with a narrow social group dents the aspirations of the rich as much as of the poor.

For poor children in an unequal affluent society, being funneled into a school for the poor means becoming part of a group within which the idea of staying on in education at older ages is not common and where a limited range of occupations are suggested to you (once you realize that footballer and pop star are unlikely).

Only three per cent of the richest one-thousandth of Americans are highly paid media and sports celebrities. That is, 3 in every 100,000 people in the United States. Far more US estate agents are rich than pop and sport stars combined. But even estate agents (realtors) make up only 4.7 per cent of the richest one-thousandth. Over 90 per cent are executives, managers, financiers and lawyers.

Why equality matters

'After executives, managers and financial professionals, the next largest groups in the top 0.1 per cent of earners were lawyers with 6.2 per cent and real estate professionals at 4.7 per cent. Media and sports figures, who are often assumed to represent a large portion of very high-income earners, collectively made up only 3 per cent.'[21]

For rich children funneled into exclusive, affluent education, the only future option often now presented is going on to further study in one of a handful of select universities and then a career in one of a very small number of well-paid occupations. You have less choice: be an executive, a manager, a financier or a lawyer. These options leave you with less choice over many things but, perhaps most importantly, they give you less choice over whom you may come to love.

Why greater equality matters for lovers

The third human age, according to William Shakespeare, is that of the lover, the years of young adulthood.[22] It is at this age that humans become most acutely sensitive as to how they are perceived by others. Some surveys find that in these years physical looks and issues of attractiveness temporarily outrank riches in how social status can be perceived. Suddenly the income and wealth of your parents is much less important than how bad your acne is and whether your overall appearance happens to match what is currently considered to be attractive.

People are mammals and almost all mammals organize themselves into groups with a little inequality inherent in the group, as well as a great deal of co-operative equality. For instance, mammals often hunt as a pack but have a pecking order. Older teenagers and younger adults are not that unlike our nearest animal cousins, great apes, in some of their grouping and ranking behavior concerning friends and acquaintances. In fact, we are all not that different from other apes, but we are often more constrained in our behaviors at both older and younger ages than we are as teenagers and young adults.

Equality matters for lovers because, in times and places of greater equality, artificial taboos on whom you might love are less frequently imposed. There are no untouchable castes in more equal societies. Under greater equality there is no significant class distinction. Women are also not looked down upon as creatures unable to make their own decisions as to whom to love or even over what they read about love.

'Would you wish your wife or servants to read *Lady Chatterley's Lover*?' is the question most well known worldwide for exposing the pomposity of a section of British society. It was asked by the prosecuting attorney in 1960 of a jury in the obscenity trial of DH Lawrence's book about a lady who falls in love with one of her many servants, a gamekeeper. The book's plot was only plausible because it was written in a time and place of great inequality (1920s England).

At times of great equality, furtive glances up and down the social spectrum at others you might fancy but must not touch are no longer taboo. Many more taboos have been broken as much greater equality has been won for people who are gay or lesbian or belong to other sexual minorities, each once considered a stigmatized or even sinful group to belong to.

All kinds of human love can be expressed more openly when rules need no longer be imposed to ensure that people who are not supposed to mix do not do so. Racial color bars to mixed marriages were only ever introduced when one racial group was made much poorer than another due to financial inequalities.

The recent rise in inequalities, as measured by income and wealth in many countries, has often had only a very small dampening effect on the more general progress towards equality in love in recent years. But,

Why equality matters

as children and young adults become more segregated by income and wealth, then opportunities to mix reduce and wealth inequalities are further exacerbated.

As wealth becomes concentrated in rich families through marriage (including now same-sex unions), you have to ignore a huge number of potential life partners in order to choose someone primarily because they come from a similar income bracket to you.

Why greater equality matters as we age

Material inequalities may have a great effect on children but they are often most keenly felt in adulthood. Shakespeare's life-stage at which people were said to be fighting for recognition, the age of the soldier, can be equated to the 'mostly out of education but not yet mid-life years' of 25-39. At the start of these years there is often great optimism. At the end it becomes more apparent where the battle has got you and how much you had to fight along the way to get there.

Many young adults, especially in more unequal countries, harbor fantasies of achieving great success. The word 'aspiration' is usually reserved for this and is often presented as if it were a good thing. But unrealistic aspirations are most likely to be held and then dashed where there is less equality, less room at the top, and where aspirations are often far greater because the rich have so much that the target for apparent success has to be set very high.

Growing up in a more equal society at more equal times, you tend to wish for things that are realistic and which also are less likely to harm others around you (if you attain them). You wish to have happiness and good health in your family, more than you wish to own and drive a series of fast 'sports' cars. You might aspire to a career which is seen as useful, rather than to earn as much money as possible.

More laudable and achievable aspirations are more common under greater equality. Egalitarians exhort the ordinary, the regular, the sustainable, the average, which can be for the (excellent and outstanding) good of all, without any of the corrosive effects of any individual having to pretend to be either excellent or outstanding. Adults also find it easier to be better parents where being a good parent is valued over being a rich parent and where fewer parents have to endure poverty.

Moving rapidly on, the fifth of Shakespeare's ages is the age of the justice, nowadays around the years 40 to 59. It is between these ages that income inequalities tend to be greatest. By age 40 in an affluent nation, your career – or lack of it – is established and your children – if you have any – are mostly born. In some of the poorest and most unequal countries of the world, it is at this point that you enter old age. If your body has been beaten down by the insults of poverty, then it is in your forties and fifties that the ramifications of the times and places you have grown up in and lived through begin most obviously to hit home. You also have a little more time to contemplate them and where you are heading next. You are supposed, by now, to be wise. One reason Shakespeare called this the age of justice is that this is the age at which a few people are usually first appointed to judge others.

In more equal countries, far fewer adults have to be actual justices of the peace because far fewer crimes are committed. Rates of imprisonment are incredibly low in almost all of the most equitable of nations, such as the Nordic countries and Japan. Imprisonment is expensive, which is why it did not become commonplace in the world until some people in some countries grew very affluent.[23] In the most equal countries you can be 10 or 20 times less likely to end up in prison as an adult partly because you are much less likely to resort to crime.

The fifth human age is also that at which we are supposed to be better at judging what is fair, but people tend to make better judges if they have been brought up and socialized in conditions of greater equality. In the country I live in and know best, England, judges are more likely than any other single profession to be drawn from the very richest strata of society. They thus have minimal experience of the lives of the people upon whom they sit in judgment and are often considered out of touch with normality.

The sixth age of life is the stage that most people in the world still don't get to complete, but it is just the first part of retirement in more affluent countries. These are the years of the 'lean and slippered pantaloon', around 60 to 74 among the affluent. In William Shakespeare's time 'pantaloon' meant an old fool. And from those Elizabethan years all the way through to the time of Queen Elizabeth II's youth, ageing was to be greatly feared and was often accompanied by hunger. There were only pensions for a tiny chosen few.

Greater equality brought the idea of retirement, of pensions by right, of minimal living standards. It is what made old age enjoyable. Predictably, in more equitable affluent countries you get to retire earlier – at 60 in Japan and 62 in France. In the most unequal of rich countries that age is currently rising, to 67 in the UK (68 soon) and in the US a huge number of elderly people have inadequate pensions to live on and have to work until they die. They have no retirement age despite the riches of their nation.

For William Shakespeare the final age was 'Sans teeth, sans eyes, sans taste, sans everything'. Sans is French (and archaic English) for without. It won't surprise you to know that the number of teeth you keep, your chances of having your cataracts fixed or your glaucoma spotted, and even your likelihood of still being able to enjoy the taste of things, to keep your senses about you and to be active and appreciated, are all much greater if you live in a society where resources are not being hoarded for themselves by a few.

It is when you come to think about how you would

like to end your days, whether you would want the younger person caring for you in your final year to resent you or respect you, that the exceptional foolishness of advocating courses of action which lead to greater inequality becomes apparent. Your money might buy you human servants and expensive medicines, but not respect nor love, or necessarily real dignity. At the grossest extreme, private health companies will have a vested interest in keeping your physical body alive as long as possible, but they will undeniably make a greater profit if you are sedated while they do it.

The final chapter of this short guide concerns how we should go about gaining greater equality but it is worth realizing that this is far from some impossible mission. It is also worth thinking, as you consider how the very richest die, often pumped full of expensive drugs, just how wide the benefits of greater equality reach.

It may surprise you, but we have been becoming more equal for quite some time – most of us, most people in the world. Gaining greater equality is not some fantasy; it has been the real-life experience of most of our parents, grandparents and their parents. That is, if you look within the countries which are home to most people, and if you take the long view and are not mesmerized by what has happened most recently.

The past is one good guide to how greater equality can be gained. Experiences of countries that are more equal are another guide. In addition, new ideas and aspirations for greater equality are constantly being created and these too are guides. Old ideals have to be defended, along with what some have already gained: pensions, social benefits, free education, healthcare, housing; a very long list in affluent countries. In poorer countries the list is often a little shorter, but it has tended to be lengthening, at least until very recently.

Greater equality matters because under it more people are treated as being fully human.

Why equality matters

1 On current attitudes to inequality and equality in London, probably the most unequal among the rich cities of the Global North, see: T Lanning and K Lawton, *Getting What We Deserve? Attitude to pay, reward and desert*, IPPR, London, 2011. The quotation is from p28. **2** Also called 'Thongs' or 'Jandals', depending on where you live. **3** All of the evidence on this is neatly summarized in Richard Wilkinson and Kate Pickett's book *The Spirit Level: Why equality is better for everyone*, Penguin, London, 2009. See equalitytrust.org.uk **4** By quintile-group-comparisons the Chinese are more equitable than the Indians, but still suffer from high rates of income inequality which, among the countries of the Global North, are only to be found in the US. **5** Giving birth is not always safer in richer countries. Compare, for example, the infant survival rates of Cuba and the US. In Cuba, income inequalities as measured between decile groups are almost five times lower than in the US. **6** UNICEF, *The State of the World's Children 2011*. **7** We can work out that fewer babies in absolute terms are born now than in the 1970s by calculating the drop as: 28% = 100 minus (100 x 1.67 x 0.43). We also know that half as many of those babies now die in their first year of life. So the number of parents who grieve the loss of a baby is now less than half the number it was in the 1970s. **8** See the table of the 26 largest rich nations sorted by income inequality in Chapter 5. Here I include affluent countries with a population of at least two million. Singapore may mostly be a small island, but it is home to over four million people. **9** Google it – that way you can learn as much or as little as you like. For those who have internet access, it is a wonderful leveler of knowledge. For those who don't, a new hurdle has been erected. **10** They might also be contested spaces dominated by the inequalities of patriarchy, but compared to the ruthlessness of many modern labor markets they are a playground (which is also a 'contested space of domination'). **11** There is a good argument to be made that: 'Fatherhood is a human social invention and patriarchy, the rule of the father, is a fundamental condition of history and of our ideas of power, authority, and of civilization itself'. See: S Kraemer, 'The origins of fatherhood: An Ancient Family Process,' *Family Process* 30(4), 1991, 377-392. **12** The latest numbers will be in: Office for National Statistics, Birth Statistics 2009, Vol 38, Palgrave Macmillan, Basingstoke, 2011 (see section on foundlings/abandoned children). There were 4 in 2004, 3 in 2006 (called 'abandoned children' by then). **13** See reference 3 above for pointers to much of the scientific evidence. **14** On attachment theories, see: C Reeves, 2007, beyondthecouch.org/1207/reeves.htm **15** O James, *The Selfish Capitalist: origins of Affluenza*, Vermilion, London, 2008. **16** O James, *Affluenza: how to be successful and stay sane*, Vermilion, London, 2007. **17** See Fig 21, D Dorling, *Injustice: why social inequality persists*, Policy Press, Bristol, 2011. **18** T Kasser, *The High Price of Materialism*, MIT Press, Cambridge, Mass, 2002. **19** M Ridley, *The Rational Optimist*, Fourth Estate, London, 2011. **20** RH Frank, *Falling Behind: How Rising Inequality Harms the Middle Class*, University of California Press, 2007. **21** On only 3% of the richest 0.1% being entertainers and sports stars, see: Peter Whoriskey, 'With executive pay, rich pull away from rest of America,' *Washington Post*, 19 Jun 2011. nin.tl/r8OdBJ **22** On the seven ages and measuring inequality by age see Bethan Thomas & Danny Dorling, *Identity in Britain: a cradle-to-grave atlas*, Policy Press, Bristol, 2007. Online examples can be found here: nin.tl/rnKheo **23** To be fair, like most things, the reasons for the rise in imprisonment are a little bit more complex. For a very complicated but great guide see: L Throness, *A Protestant Purgatory: Theological origins of the penitentiary act, 1779*, Ashgate, Aldershot, 2008.

2 What is equality?

Statistics show the extreme inequality between continents and nations. But equality is well worth pursuing. Not only are humans happier and healthier when they are more equal, but more equal societies offer greater social mobility – as well as reducing population growth.

'All human beings are born free and equal in dignity and rights.'
Universal Declaration of Human Rights,
1948, article 1.

THE BASIC THRUST of this *No-Nonsense Guide* is that human beings are happier and healthier the more equal they are, and that this is borne out by looking at statistics from all over the world today – as well as by surveying the whole of human history. My view comes from lots of other people's views – I didn't think these things up by myself.

Equality means being afforded the same rights, dignity and freedoms as other people. These include rights to access resources, the dignity of being seen as able and the freedom to choose what to make of your life on an equal footing with others. Believing that we are all quite equal in what we could do is very far from suggesting that we would all do much the same were we more equal.[1]

Although leftwing and green politicians tend to advocate greater equality more vocally and rightwing and fascist ones might join parties to oppose it, equality is not the preserve of any political label. Great inequality has been sustained or increased under systems labeled as socialist and communist. Some free-market systems have seen equalities grow and the playing field become more level. More anarchistic systems with smaller or non-existent states can be equitable or inequitable.

Advocates of inequality tend to churn out uninspiring nonsense about how doing others down will somehow help all in the end. Or they suggest, with no evidence, that under greater equality everyone is less happy. They also accuse egalitarians of being advocates of uniformity. In fact, the opposite is the case. In times and places of greater equality we are (and have been) freer to each choose our individual role and how we can each contribute best. Under great inequality, the vast majority of people are condemned to lives of quite uniform poverty, while most of the rich are uniformly drab in their ignorance of alternatives. Under great inequality, people lose individuality by status seeking, aping their betters, and worrying more about how they are perceived. There is far more variety when we are more equal.

Egalitarians get the most laughs

Chapter 1 began by employing comedy, and in particular some well-known sayings attributed to the actor Mae West to explain why equality matters. Comedy and what is considered humorous varies greatly from place to place and time to time, but there are some common variants. One of these is laughing at the follies of those who are rich or who, in some way, otherwise appear to get above themselves. Sometimes nothing needs to be said other than to quote back a person's words. Here is an example which is interesting because, despite the person quoted being fully aware of the need to be modest, they still manage to slip up. This example shows just how easy it is to become the object of humor designed to promote equality:

'My parents didn't buy me loads of stuff as a child and I've been taught not to take things for granted and be smart about how I spend my money. I still have the

same car I've had since I was a teenager. It is a grey Land Rover Freelander.'[2]

(Lily Collins, daughter of the musician Phil Collins, aged 22 when making these comments in 2011)

Whether you find Lily's words funny depends not only on your sense of humor but also on whether you know what a 'Land Rover Freelander' is and realize it is quite an expensive car. It also helps if you live somewhere where teenagers do occasionally drive but are rarely given Freelanders – let alone see the fact that they have not replaced their car in four years as some kind of evidence of their frugality.

In the social world Lily Collins lives in, not updating your car is frugality. In the wider world she shares, her words are quoted back by others to say 'at least realize her folly'. More widely still, her words would not appear particularly funny as any adult – especially any woman – having any access to a car is a rarity in much of the world, whether it's expensive or not, and whether they are aged 22 or 62. Chastizing humor of this kind tends only to work among people with similar experiences, and hence works best when and where equality is greater.

A comic needs to establish a rapport with her audience if they are to share a joke – we do not communicate well with people we think are either beneath or above us. Similarly, when writing a book (like this) for a stranger to read, it is best done by treating that stranger as an equal. People who believe they are superior to most others find it hard not to betray their disdain when they write, or speak, or joke.

Lily may never read the satirical magazine in which her words were lampooned, but others, including some she associates with, will. As rich people become older, they learn to be careful over what they say about their wealth. Younger mammals are almost always more foolish than older mammals. What the normal degree of equality is has to be learned; it is not ingrained. Different degrees of equality are also normal at different times and in different places.

In the distant past, after a natural disaster, it may well have been the selfish that were more likely to survive. Otherwise why should selfishness itself have survived? Alternatively, should you be born into times when society is better organized, then your parents may try to bring you up to be less selfish, and you might well fit better into normal human society. As Lily went on to say later in that interview: *'My mum and dad have kept me down to earth and very focused.'*

You get on better in a society when you are seen to fit in, to be more humble and understanding. Lily's parents may have tried to instill such down-to-earth behavior in Lily because it's a very old instinct to behave well – for good reasons of human survival. However, they may also have encouraged her to be focused because they know she'll have to compete under circumstances where very few are awarded the quantities of wealth that her parents have received.

All are not equal – and it is in our minds that the greatest differences between us are found, not in how clever we are but in what we know. The apparently most sharp-witted and knowledgeable person, the one who can always find a fact or phrase to defend their argument, may simply through accident of birth have been brought up to believe untruths and to see themselves or their race, family, sex or caste as superior (or indeed as inferior).

If you have been fortunate enough not to have been brought up to believe in inequality as a good thing, then perhaps you should not scoff at those who (through no fault of their own) find it much harder to understand our inherent equality. However, that does not mean that you can't have a laugh over their ignorance.

It is well worth asking why comedy has (for as long as it has existed) been used to put down those who get above themselves, to pour scorn on advocates of difference and to upturn social conventions of hierarchy. However, it is also unfortunately used to laugh at those who are less fortunate, different or accident prone.

As times and places change, all our understanding changes. What we might have thought was solid truth can melt into irrelevance. Advocates for greater equality in one era can quickly sound out of date and unthinking a few generations later, especially where progress has been made. What is funny also changes quickly over time, but underlying those changes in humor are changes in belief systems, especially beliefs about how equal or different we inherently are.

Inequality worldwide

Beliefs also vary greatly between places concerning what resources it is thought fair that people should have access to, especially the richest and the poorest in any one society. One group can be seen as able and treated with dignity in one country, but not in another, at exactly the same time. There are wide variations in the freedom to choose what to make of your life between different places in the world, and these are often very different from what is commonly suggested.

Across Western Europe, welfare states (which would be better termed social states) were constructed in the aftermath of World War Two. This is partly why the poorest tenth of Germans now live on 50 per cent more than the poorest tenth of people in North America while in Sweden they live on much nearer to twice as much (see the Table below).[3] It was the US government's Marshall Plan aid which helped construct these social states. Similarly, the US undertook social engineering in post-war Japan, which is why income inequalities are so low in that country today.

What is equality?

Although the US has been responsible for acts that have helped secure greater equalities elsewhere in the affluent world, in recent decades the US government has pursued a different course domestically, intervening less to redress inequalities. As a result, people's life chances in North America (as reflected through income) are now almost as unequal as those in Africa, as the table below shows. North America might be much richer but the 90:10 ratio column, which shows the ratio of the income of the richest

Income inequality by continent and in selected countries					
			Annual income in comparable US$		
Region or country	Population (millions)	90:10 ratio	poorest 10th	median	richest 10th
World	6123	13.5	1800	6000	24300
Africa	819	21.6	400	1600	8300
Asia	3643	11.1	1200	3700	13600
Latin America and the Caribbean	530	58.3	600	4000	33500
North America	322	17.7	6400	25800	113600
Europe	717	9.5	5100	14900	48200
Oceania	93	15.2	2400	9000	36500
Germany	82	6.3	9700	24000	61400
Sweden	9	4.7	11100	23900	52600
Japan	128	4.1	12500	25000	51000

Note: 90:10 ratio is the mean average income of the person in the richest tenth of the population divided by the mean average for all households in the poorest tenth. This remains the most up-to-date global data. The figures for Japan have been independently verified by the author and colleagues.

Source: United Nations Human Development report 2004 and Worldmapper (table 14 of the UNDP report which maps 149 and 150 are based on). Although more up-to-date figures are available for some countries for most these are still the most recent surveys. Figures are rounded. Population figures are shown for shortly after the year 2000 to be most comparable with the majority of countries' income data.

tenth to that of the poorest tenth of the population, is almost as high as in the African continent. Canada is much less unequal than the US but the sheer size of its southern neighbor dominates the overall record for the North American continent, which also includes Mexico and the Bahamas.

The US also supported dictatorships in Latin America and the Caribbean for much of the 20th century, which contributed to South America being the most unequal continent by the millennium. The region's countries are now, however, free from military dictatorship and in many cases have recently undergone social revolutions. These revolutions may have been produced by the very high levels of inequality. What is certain is that they are now combating inequality and, in consequence, it is very likely that the 90:10 ratio of 58 shown in the table is now falling. The final chapter of this *No-Nonsense Guide* looks at some of the ways in which greater equality is gained, not least as a counter-reaction to growing inequality.

Some might look at the above table and think that the best continent to live in is North America because it is there that the highest incomes are found. However, despite rhetoric about the 'American Dream', membership of the richest group in US society is largely determined by how rich your parents were when you were born, and not by your own efforts. The US has one of the lowest rates of social mobility among all nations in the rich world. A child born poor in the US is more likely to die poor than in any other affluent country. The graph overleaf demonstrates that there is a strong correlation between social mobility and income inequality, with the US losing out on both counts.

Each of the countries for which there was comparable data are represented by a dot in this graph. When income inequality is high that dot is drawn further to the right, when it is low it is drawn towards the left. Where social mobility is high, so that a parent's

What is equality?

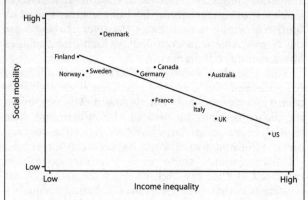

Social mobility is higher in more equal countries

Source: Intergenerational income mobility data from: J Blanden, Centre for Economic Performance, LSE, Paper No CEEDP0111, 2009. Via: equalitytrust.org.uk.

Note: This figure has been redrawn from one appearing on the Equality Trust website which was first drawn by Kate Pickett and Richard Wilkinson in 2009 and which has now been redrawn using the most recent data, showing an even closer relationship between the two variables than seen before.[4]

occupation has less bearing on a child's occupation, the dot is drawn high. The fact that almost all the dots are drawn very near to the straight line demonstrates just how closely related social mobility and income inequality are. Each influences the other. The UK, falling a little way below the line, has even lower social mobility than its income inequality would suggest, possibly a hangover from its infamously class-ridden society. In Canada, meanwhile, the deviation from the trend is in the opposite direction, but even in these two countries, which fitted the trend least well in 2009, the two social statistics remain very closely related.

People on a medium income of $25,800 can feel quite poor in the US when those above them have so much. The average person in the US might be able to buy slightly more food and clothes than the average German, Swede or Japanese, but that tends to mean that they eat a little more, get a little fatter, shop a little more and throw their clothes away a little more often as compared with the average in more equitable affluent countries.

The right to equal treatment

Human beings appear to have quarreled for millennia over the extent to which their inherent equality is self-evident, or to be disputed. At various times and places, greater equality has been won and, at other times, previous gains have been lost.

Egalitarianism encompasses a range of different beliefs. It can mean simply that all people should be treated equally or it can assert that humans are quite equal in potential, in character, and in intelligence. The more modern egalitarianism (the latter) has been boosted by more and more research suggesting that people's potential for achievement does not vary greatly.[5] The more old-fashioned egalitarianism of equal treatment, while assuming very different potentials, is still greatly relevant in that very few people receive equal treatment even today.

Over time and in different places notions of equality change. Equality is always disputed. What is equal treatment and potential are things to be argued over. This *No-Nonsense Guide* is partly about that argument. It is written in the belief that most people should be treated equally and suggests that, where this is not the case, we should move towards greater equality rather than away from it. We should aspire to equal treatment before the law, at school, in the labor market, in recreation – across the whole of life.

Most of the easily available histories of ideas about equality begin with how, between two and three millennia ago, Athenians and others developed concepts of equality before the law, of respect and of free speech (as long as you were male, local and not a slave). These histories tend to start with Greek origins not because the Greeks were the first to discuss equality but because no other origin closer to Western Europe can be found. They go on to contrast the English, French and German ideas of men such as Thomas Hobbes, Jean-Jacques Rousseau and Karl Marx.[6] Women are hardly mentioned.

Yet in any history of equality, the position of women should be the starting-point. Until very recently, most women in the world would, on average, give birth to as many as six or eight children (or even more), most of whom would die before they themselves could become parents. The graph opposite shows that this is still the case in a few very poor countries.

Today, across the vast majority of the world, including India and China, it is now much more normal to have three or fewer children, but there is surprising variation among the most affluent countries. It is partly because childbirth, upbringing and child protection dominated so many women's lives until recently that (mostly dead) men's thoughts still so dominate the general literature on equality.

To understand the graph opposite you have to realize that every circle represents a country, and each circle has an area proportional to that country's population. Circles are placed towards the right-hand side of the graph when average annual incomes are higher. Meanwhile, the more children the average woman gives birth to, the higher the circle is placed up the graph.

Imagine almost all the circles in the graph being in the top left-hand corner, the space where average incomes are low and fertility is high. That is where most of them were a century ago. Then, as median incomes rose and the circles moved towards the right, education became more widespread, infant mortality was reduced, women's rights were won and contraception became more common. As a result,

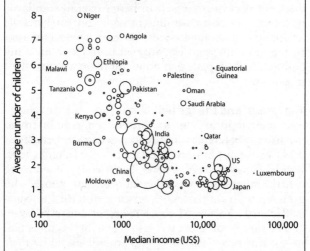

Income (US$) and average number of children

Note: The Y axis is average numbers of babies per woman and the X axis is median income in comparable US$ by year on a log scale. Circle area is proportional to the population of each country.

Source: United Nations Human Development Report and Worldmapper. Figures are for around the year 2000, as data from some regions is often very out-of-date.

fertility fell.

A very strong contemporary argument for the benefits of greater equality is to consider how it has altered the life chances of women in recent decades. Those gains may have partly been made following other emancipations, including liberation from formal slavery, winning greater employment rights and universal free secondary education for all children. Except where there is a short-lived and poorly shared-out oil bonanza, such as in Equatorial Guinea, it was the winning of such rights that made it possible for a country to have a median average annual income in excess of $10,000 per person a year. But over that

kind of an income, as the graph shows, greater wealth
does not necessarily result in better overall standards
of living – in this case illustrated by no further falls
in fertility as women choose to have fewer children.
In the more unequal US, women have twice as many
children as in Japan, and many more on average than
in Europe.

The 'great' and the 'gifted'

The contemporary 'great writers' on equality who
are usually referenced today were generally privileged
men. Those not born into great privilege (such as John
Rawls, Gerry Cohen or Peter Townsend) tended to be
a little more egalitarian in outlook than those who
grew up with rather less experience of hardship (such
as Richard Tawney, Michael Young or Amartya Sen).

The sample of 'great writers on equality' is too small
to test this theory that they too are influenced by their
backgrounds but it is interesting to ponder on the
possibility. The differences in their views are not that
great, but they tend to be constricted in their thinking
by the times in which they were born and brought up –
like all of us.

Richard Tawney, for example, who wrote a book
titled *Equality* in the 1930s, had been sent as a young
child to board at the famous English boys' private
school from which the name of the game of Rugby
derives. Could Richard Tawney have imagined himself
going to school with girls as well as boys? A few years
before he died, Rugby School started admitting girls
at the age of 16. Tawney was progressive enough
that he might have imagined girls being allowed to
attend his school. He began an organization called the
Workers' Educational Association. Today this might
be seen as a patronizing idea, but at the time it was a
near-revolutionary concept. I wonder if he could have
imagined going to the same school as all the other
children living around the town of Rugby, rather than

to an élitist private school, and yet still have ended up being taken seriously as a published writer about equality and being appointed as a university professor – which is my own situation now. I doubt he would have believed it, and yet it is a sign of how much we have advanced towards equality over the last century or so. I wonder how much that I currently believe will be found to be mistaken by the time I die...

The right to equal treatment was historically first won by those just beneath the king, then progressively won by those just beneath them, and so on down. The right to equal treatment is most commonly lost when a few from above take it away from many more of those below them. From political coups at the very top to regressive legislation reducing the freedoms of poor migrants, there are as many ways to lose these rights as there are ways to win them.

The kind of private school Richard Tawney went to as a child is, rather confusingly, called a public school in Britain because, when such schools were created in 1567, they extended access to education to the public – albeit still only to a tiny minority. 'Public schools' were thus originally a progressive force, a creation which ever so slightly increased levels of equality. Today these are the most exclusive and expensive private schools. Almost all of them still hold charitable status and so avoid paying taxes because they are meant to be doing some kind of 'public good' (which was the case in 1567 but was much less so by 1967).

It is not only institutions that can begin as advocates of greater equality and end up as bastions of privilege and prejudice; entire ways of thinking can become similarly skewed. For example, religions that start with increasing respect for other people can be perverted into disrespecting people who do not adhere to their particular faith.

Equality is not a state that is achieved permanently. It is something that is always being fought for, defended, won and lost. We are never fully equal or truly unequal. We are always becoming more or less equal in many different ways. It is almost always the case that when we become less equal we collectively suffer. As Richard Tawney pointed out to his fellow English intellectuals in the 1930s, what he called *social energy* is lost when strict inequalities are imposed.

We only become more equal in fits and starts, and often lose the rights we have previously gained. We need to be constantly reminded of the benefits of greater equality. That is because we are so similar in our physiology and ability and none of us is particularly superior. Most of us can only really think of one thing at a time, there are limits to intelligence, to how complex a concept we can grasp – for all of us, but when we are treated more equally we work together far better.

There is currently dispute in academic debate as to whether all of us have it in us to do well or whether there are some especially gifted children which in a more meritocratic society we would search out at an early age and give extra succor to. There is evidence of some groups having greater propensities for particular kinds of mental manipulations and this patterned variation in particular cognitive ability may even run in families.[7,8]

Nevertheless, I fall squarely on the side of that debate that does not find any compelling evidence for there being 'alpha' children, all-round winners, as they were chillingly described in Aldous Huxley's 1932 novel *Brave New World*. I think it is only because too many have forgotten the 1930s that this debate has now re-emerged.

Occasionally one or two individuals come out seeming better than others – a great leader, great mind or great athlete. At other times, people lament the lack of great leaders, minds or athletes. What we too rarely do is recognize the circumstances in which apparent greatness emerges. In hindsight, particular politicians come to be painted as inspirational. They usually had the good fortune of contemporary social trends already moving in the direction they advocated, but we find it easier to ascribe agency to individuals than to the times they lived through and the groups they belonged to.

We should be better at spotting the importance of circumstance, but instead we are constantly duped by celebrity – and by arguments in support of inequality. However, we are more often and more easily duped in this way when we live in places and at times of greater inequality. This is because we become a little more able under greater equality, and a little less capable when we are not treated as equals.

Standing up for equality

This *No-Nonsense Guide to Equality* keeps returning to inequality because it is so hard to avoid doing so when discussing the benefits of greater equality. It is similar to those who promote the benefits of taking exercise and refer constantly to what happens if you do not.

Although many previous generations have discovered the benefits of greater equality, and many times have committed their ideas to print or even religious decree, in much of the world in recent years teaching about the benefits of equality has diminished. The major benefit of greater equality is the most obvious one – less inequality.

A small minority of very rich people have in recent decades funded organizations and individuals who promote greater inequality and try to make a virtue of it. These apostles of inequality suggest the people need not work together but that (somehow) bitter competition will result in a better world for all.[9] As a result, there are many books written that advocate inequality, or at least see it as a necessary evil, and many others that counter these by explaining the harm caused by inequality, but there are far fewer books that explain the simple benefits of greater equality.

At the core of egalitarianism is the belief that people should be both treated and understood as equals. We are not fundamentally different because of any group we happen to have been assigned to, whether on the basis of class, caste, gender, race, religion, disability... any group.

I am dyslexic, which makes me a slow reader and causes errors in my writing (and gives the editor of this book plenty of work). You might not have this disability, but perhaps you cannot run very fast. Neither makes us second-rate people. We are just different. Furthermore, you may read quickly but miss the point, and I might run fast but in the wrong direction. People do vary on how they score compared to each other in the assessment of measurable skills, but, to be measurable, a skill has to be very basic, such as reading a list or running fast. The less basic the skill, the harder it is to measure how good we are at it and even to agree on what 'good' means – as in judging what is great poetry or dance.

Ideas about equality naturally change with the times. At first a small slight might be considered objectionable, but at a later date it might be recognized as a larger wrong, then as abhorrent, finally even as evil. Egalitarians currently find many things abhorrent, including slavery, racism, hatred of women (and men), and great divides between rich and poor. In future they may find the debilitating effects of much of the testing and grading of children we currently engage in to be abhorrent, but not yet.

Over time, egalitarians' field of reference tends to expand to include previously ignored groups. Children and elderly people are now beginning to be considered as, in many circumstances, unfairly treated because of their group membership. The same applies to people who are disabled, including those with a congenital disability; and those with mild learning difficulties.

As I was writing this book, a British Conservative MP suggested that disabled people should be paid less than the minimum wage so as to encourage an employer to offer them a job. The Conservative Prime Minister, David Cameron, distanced himself from this politician, which indicates how social norms can quickly change. British Conservative leaders in the recent past might well have publicly agreed with such an MP.

Very rapid gains are often made in securing greater equality, as has been the case for groups differentiated by their sexuality in recent years, at least in Western societies. That same Conservative Prime Minister, David Cameron, held a party for lesbian, gay, bisexual and transgender (LGBT) sports stars in June 2011 – something that would have been unthinkable for a Conservative leader even 20 years before.[10]

Similarly, and hardly surprisingly, previously hard won equalities can suddenly be lost. For example, it turns out that David Cameron's chief political advisor was advocating reducing maternity pay at the very same time as the liberal summer sports party was being staged. If it were not the case that equalities can be lost as well as gained, the human world would by now be a far more equitable place.

A good example of an equality lost is the equal right of all to travel. Prior to World War One, almost everyone in the world had the freedom to travel to anywhere in the world. Most did not have the means but they were not prevented from crossing borders simply because of who they were and where they came from. Within a very few years, passports were introduced, followed very shortly by immigration controls and suddenly freedom of movement was lost for the vast majority of people in the world. For the minority who hold the right passport and a sufficient bank balance, meanwhile, the barriers to cheap and fast travel have come down, allowing them to travel to the other end of the earth even for a brief holiday.

What is equality?

Seen in the round, therefore, travel is an example of a field of activity where there has been a rapid increase in inequality and a great loss of freedom.

Passport controls exemplify how increases in inequalities can be argued for, rationalized and achieved. They are themselves a product of growing inequality. Usually, through unfair terms of trade following colonization, people in some countries became much richer as compared with people in other countries. Given this, there would be a natural tendency for people in poorer countries to migrate to the places where their ancestors' wealth had been gathered. It is to stop this migration and defend rich countries' privileged place within an unequal world order that immigration and passport controls have been introduced. To protect the amassed wealth of a few everyone must now seek permission to travel.

Why women's rights change everything

Conversely, a gain in equality in one area can lead to unanticipated progress elsewhere. Greater rights for women, for instance, almost always result in fewer children being born and often more equality amongst the subsequent smaller generation. This is one reason why this chapter keeps returning to fertility as a quantitative example.

Many people worry about there being too many people in the world, but, as people become better off, it is those in more equitable affluent societies who have the fewest babies. And, as we shall see later, those children each tend to consume less, since people growing up in more equitable rich countries feel less need to go shopping.

Greater equality is partly greater freedom from fear. In a more equitable society, you need have less fear over the future of your children and over your own ability to prosper in old age. In a more equitable society, far fewer children are very poor and so far fewer die in childhood. The lower the rate of infant and child mortality, the fewer children adults tend to have. Similarly, in a more economically equitable society your financial well-being in old age does not depend upon having more children who might look after you.

Greater equality results in more stability and could well be one reason behind the recent rapid global decline in human fertility. Income equality in most of the Western world rose as family sizes fell from 1880 to 1980. Across North America, the average number of children per woman had fallen to its minimum of 1.79 by the end of that period, but rose thereafter as social inequalities increased.

The table below shows the average number of babies born worldwide and in each continent every five years from 1950 onwards. It shows how fertility is now lowest in the most equitable of affluent continents (Europe) and highest in the second most unequal and the poorest of continents (Africa). Thus one of the widest benefits of egalitarianism can be a world approaching human population stability.

We should be careful to celebrate the gains in equality that have recently been made. Far more is written on the global rise in income and wealth inequality and the growing gaps between different social classes of people than, for example, on the closing gap in income inequalities between countries in recent years.[11]

Women form the largest group of people to have recently won much greater equality in most countries of the world. Again, because of our attention to the harm done by inequalities, many readers' immediate reaction to such a statement might be to respond that almost everywhere there is so much further yet to go before women are treated as equals to men. Yet only a century ago, in most of the newly industrializing world, the position of women was little different from that of slaves.

What is equality?

Total fertility: Children born to each woman, 1950-2010

Region	1950-1955	1955-1960	1960-1965	1965-1970	1970-1975	1975-1980	1980-1985	1985-1990	1990-1995	1995-2000	2000-2005	2005-2010
World	4.95	4.89	4.91	4.85	4.45	3.84	3.59	3.39	3.04	2.79	2.62	2.52
Africa	6.60	6.66	6.71	6.68	6.67	6.57	6.38	6.07	5.62	5.23	4.94	4.64
Asia	5.82	5.58	5.58	5.61	5.00	4.05	3.69	3.43	2.97	2.65	2.41	2.28
Latin America and the Caribbean	5.86	5.91	5.96	5.53	5.02	4.47	3.93	3.42	3.02	2.73	2.53	2.30
North America	3.33	3.64	3.36	2.55	2.05	1.80	1.79	1.87	1.96	1.93	1.99	2.03
Europe	2.65	2.64	2.56	2.35	2.17	1.98	1.89	1.82	1.57	1.42	1.43	1.53
Oceania	3.81	4.02	4.00	3.57	3.30	2.74	2.57	2.49	2.49	2.45	2.41	2.49

Source: United Nations, Department of Economic and Social Affairs, Population Division: World Population Prospects DEMOBASE extract, 2011.

The figure opposite contains two graphs. In the first graph the continents of the world are each shown by a circle drawn in proportion to their population. Three low-fertility countries are also shown: Germany, Sweden (the smallest circle) and Japan. The highest circle in the top graph is Africa, because the vertical axis of the graph is the average number of children each woman gives birth to. The circle drawn furthest to the right is Latin America and the Caribbean because the horizontal axis is of income inequality, which here is the ratio between the income of the best-off and the worst-off tenth. Countries are shown in the lower graph. In general, the more equitable a country or continent is, the lower the fertility. A slowly declining human population would have a fertility rate of around or just under two children per woman.

The second graph shows exactly the same data as in the top panel, but now for all countries rather than just three. There is a wide range of fertility amongst unequal countries, but more equal countries all appear to have low fertility. The US, which makes up most of North America, is now largely obscured on this second graph in the figure. There isn't space to

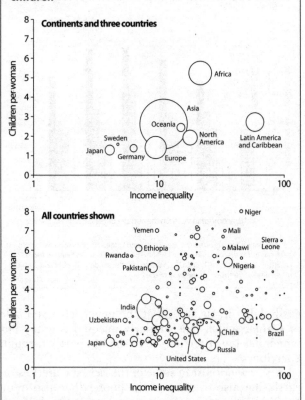

Worldwide income inequality and average number of children

Continents and three countries

(Y-axis: Children per woman, 0 to 8; X-axis: Income inequality, 1 to 100, log scale)

Africa, Asia, Oceania, North America, Latin America and Caribbean, Sweden, Japan, Germany, Europe

All countries shown

(Y-axis: Children per woman, 0 to 8; X-axis: Income inequality, 1 to 100, log scale)

Niger, Yemen, Mali, Sierra Leone, Ethiopia, Malawi, Rwanda, Nigeria, Pakistan, India, Uzbekistan, China, Japan, Russia, Brazil, United States

Note: 'According to the United Nations Economic Commission for Latin America, the decile ratio (share of total income for the top 10 per cent of wage earners divided by the bottom 10 per cent) in Latin America was 45 to 1, while that of Cuba was only 4 to 1.' (en.wikipedia.org/wiki/EconomyofCuba).

Source: Data is from UNDP report 2004 and Worldmapper using table 14 of the UNDP report. Income inequality is the ratio of the income of the richest tenth to the poorest tenth and is drawn on a log scale as the horizontal axis of each graph. The vertical axis of each is average lifetime number of live babies born per woman.

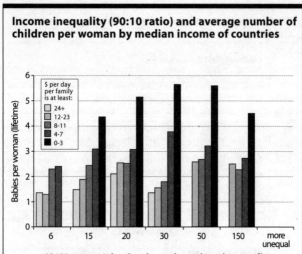

Income inequality (90:10 ratio) and average number of children per woman by median income of countries

Y-axis: Babies per woman (lifetime)

Legend: $ per day per family is at least:
- 24+
- 12-23
- 8-11
- 4-7
- 0-3

X-axis: 6, 15, 20, 30, 50, 150, more unequal

90:10 income ratio less than the number under each group of bars

Source: Data is from around the year 2000 from United Nations sources. Height of each bar is the average number of children born to all women living in those countries with the median income indicated by the shade of the bar and with the inequality range shown at the base of the bar.

easily label it, tucked up at the upper left hand side of China, which is a similarly unequal country but which has lower fertility than the US, partly through coercion.

It is now not just in some of the richest countries on earth, but also in some of the poorer (but also more equitable) countries, that women have fewer children. In the bar chart above, affluent countries are colored the lightest grey, and poorest countries the darkest. Countries are grouped in bars, however, according to their levels of income inequality, not their wealth – the number below each group of bars shows the inequality ratio. In the first group, for example, the best-off tenth of the population receives less than six times the income of the poorest tenth.

Fertility in the world is lowest – at around 1.3 children per woman – in those very affluent countries that are most equitable. Very poor countries tend also to be very unequal countries and to have high fertility rates. Greater prosperity and greater equality tend to be accompanied by lower overall fertility. When women are given more rights, more education and more money, fertility falls and overall equality rises.

Winning greater equality may be a precursor to achieving higher living standards (the American Revolution being a key example). Today, of the most equitable group of countries, none fall within the poorest category included in the key of the figure above. Of the most inequitable groups of countries, the graph shows that none have median incomes over $24 a day. There are no lightest-colored bars in the two right-hand clusters. More equitable countries tend to have both better-off citizens and more sustainable birth rates. When combined with higher living standards, greater equality appears to be driving the slowdown in the growth of global human population.

1 A Offer, *The Challenge of Affluence: Self-Control and Well-Being in the United States and Britain since 1950*, Oxford University Press, 2006. 2 *Private Eye* 1289, 27 May 2011. Lily Collins' words in full can be found at: nin.tl/mUFuBo 3 New Zealand had introduced a social state and great equality before the Second World War. For more information start with: nin.tl/p26F3w 4 See equalitytrust.org.uk/why/evidence/social-mobility 5 I tried to summarize this collection of research, including the results of many hundreds of recent studies, in: Danny Dorling, *Injustice: why social inequality persists*, Policy Press, Bristol, 2011. 6 JC Myers, *The Politics of Equality*, Zed Books, London, 2010. 7 G Davies et al, 'Genome-wide association studies establish that human intelligence is highly heritable and polygenic,' *Molecular Psychiatry*, 10.1038/mp.2011.85, 2011. 8 G Davey Smith, 'Epidemiology, epigenetics and the "Gloomy Prospect": embracing randomness in population health research and practice,' *International Journal of Epidemiology* 40, 2011. 9 M Ridley, *The Rational Optimist*, Fourth Estate, London, 2011. 10 publicservice.co.uk/news_story.asp?id=16683 11 This claim was first made in 1999. Whether it is true depends almost entirely on how accurate current income estimates are for China, and to a lesser extent in India. See Glenn Firebaugh, 'Empirics of World Income Inequality', *American Journal of Sociology*, 104, 1999.

3 Winning greater equality
– and losing it

We only win greater equality by standing up for our rights – and rights we take for granted now had once to be fought for. As recently as the 1970s, the people of Canada, the US and the UK were more equal than they had ever been in history – yet they have since pursued policies that have returned inequality to 1930s levels. Despite globalization, countries still choose the road to equality or inequality – as China and India are choosing now.

'We hold these truths to be self-evident, that all men are created equal, that they are endowed by their Creator with certain unalienable Rights, that among these are Life, Liberty and the pursuit of Happiness.'
US Declaration of Independence, 1776

SMALL GROUPS OF PEOPLE can meet and talk and send representatives from their group to meet representatives of other groups, say in a 'house of representatives'. There is, of course, great scope here for the representatives to become detached from those they are supposed to be representing, especially if the process involves a whole hierarchy of groups.

Yet even this clumsy mechanism has resulted in greater equality being gained – and continues to do so. The US 'House of Representatives' first met formally three years after the 1776 declaration of intent (Independence) was drawn up as a result of just such a small group meeting.

The men who drafted and signed the world's most famous document advocating greater equality included many who owned slaves and a large majority who would not consider women as men's equals. Nevertheless, they signed a declaration which is still held in awe today (see box overleaf). Having declared that all men (it was 1776) were created equal and that democratic government was essential, those now known as the 'Founding Fathers' of the United States went on to list a huge number of insults they were suffering, and laid them all down at the door of the main advocate of inequality of their day – George III, the King of England.

King George, in response to the insubordination of those he saw as beneath him, ordered his troops to destroy the first House of Representatives. They did this in 1814 when the first White House was also burned to the ground, but greater equality won out. Today, on its website, the officials of the US House of Representatives celebrate key gains in greater equality, writing that:

'The House's first African-American member was elected in 1870. The first Hispanic member took office in 1877, the first woman member in 1917, the first Asian-American member in 1957, and the first African-American woman member in 1969. In 2007, Representative Nancy Pelosi of California was elected as the first woman Speaker of the House.'[1]

Nowhere are losses of equality listed as achievements.

Greater equality is often won only once great insult has been recognized. Future egalitarians may look back on us today and ask why we did not consider children's rights more fully. They may wonder why we did not value more highly the rights of those at the end of life, of prisoners of war, of criminals, of people considered deranged or simple, or of others whom we are unable yet to recognize as a disregarded group today.

Equality is a process, not an end, which is why in this book I so often precede it with the word 'greater'. Other groups are constantly being recognized as fully human, which is usually the first step towards greater equality being won. People do not easily bomb, torture or starve others they recognize as being human, as being like them. We have to strive for greater equality endlessly, not to create a world of pure equality, but just to get our basic rights accepted as normal.

The unanimous Declaration of the 13 united States of America, 4 July 1776

'When in the Course of human events it becomes necessary for one people to dissolve the political bands which have connected them with another and to assume among the powers of the earth, the separate and equal station to which the Laws of Nature and of Nature's God entitle them, a decent respect to the opinions of mankind requires that they should declare the causes which impel them to the separation.

'We hold these truths to be self-evident, that all men are created equal, that they are endowed by their Creator with certain unalienable Rights, that among these are Life, Liberty and the pursuit of Happiness. — That to secure these rights, Governments are instituted among Men, deriving their just powers from the consent of the governed, — That whenever any Form of Government becomes destructive of these ends, it is the Right of the People to alter or to abolish it, and to institute new Government, laying its foundation on such principles and organizing its powers in such form, as to them shall seem most likely to effect their Safety and Happiness. Prudence, indeed, will dictate that Governments long established should not be changed for light and transient causes; and accordingly all experience hath shewn that mankind are more disposed to suffer, while evils are sufferable than to right themselves by abolishing the forms to which they are accustomed. But when a long train of abuses and usurpations, pursuing invariably the same Object evinces a design to reduce them under absolute Despotism, it is their right, it is their duty, to throw off such Government, and to provide new Guards for their future security. — Such has been the patient sufferance of these Colonies; and such is now the necessity which constrains them to alter their former Systems of Government. The history of the present King of Great Britain is a history of repeated injuries and usurpations, all having in direct object the establishment of an absolute Tyranny over these States.' ∎

The Declaration proceeds to list multiple examples of the King's tyranny, requiring some 28 paragraphs to contain all the insults. The full document can be accessed at ushistory.org/declaration/document/

How one gain can lead to another

In English-speaking countries we only now celebrate the words of the US Declaration of Independence because the insurgents won. This declaration of the 'Oppressed' labels the original inhabitants of the Americas as 'merciless Indian Savages'. Often every group that sees itself as oppressed is simultaneously oppressing another group below them (Black, female or Native American in this case). Inequalities can create further inequalities as downtrodden people so often kick those beneath them.

It has been suggested that reacting to being dominated by trying to dominate others is a very old human trait. It is even seen in chimpanzees – when a dominant adult kicks a subordinate adult, the kicked animal bows down in supplication to the superior, almost as if praying, while simultaneously kicking an adult who is even lower down the order. The trait in apes is called 'bicycling' because the middle animal appears to be riding a bike as it kicks backwards.

Bicycling behavior can be cited as evidence that we are not innately more disposed to share, or to be kind or co-operative. These traits we share with chimpanzees suggest that we have a long common past of hoarding and excluding others. It is hard to disentangle but, given what we know from psychoanalytic observations about infant and toddler states of mind, we should recognize that humans can be appallingly greedy, destructive and envious mammals as well as sublimely generous, curious and playful ones. The psychologist Sigmund Freud suggested that it is the task of civilization to contain one and promote the other and anthropologist Christopher Boehm says it was much the same for ancient societies.[2]

Even if we all were to gain greater equality, 'bicycling' would not be eliminated in the brave new world. We should not be naïve about human nature, including our own. It is also worth asking where the political rage some of us hold against promoters of inequality comes from. We in turn may be partly trying to kick down, even as we kick back.

You can observe bicycling today if you work in an open-plan office or overhear business conversations people have on their mobile phones on trains. Very often the person whose half conversation you can overhear is either bullying or being bullied. You can tell if the man opposite you in the train is being chided by his boss on the phone. He is subservient in the relationship if all he offers by way of conversation is apology and excuses between being forced to listen to long periods of tirade. In my experience, often after the conversation ends the man then phones his underling to 'tear a strip' off him or her. Or he phones his wife to complain about his children or some other aspect of life. Or he snaps at the person offering to sell him a coffee from the trolley.

The British have been world leaders at bullying and the practice is still more common in its schools than in any other affluent nation (although in recent years it has been rapidly reducing as greater equalities have been won). Britain partly maintained its enormous world empire through chains of bullying. These chains stretched from the playing fields of Eton to the slums of Calcutta (now Kolkata).

Indians celebrate the anniversary of 15 August 1947 because that was when they finally secured independence. In contrast to the Indians and the Americans, the English have no date to celebrate or clear (written) constitution or bill of rights worth an annual remembering because almost every insurrection within Britain was put down, and even those that were not, as in 1649 or 1689, represented a substitution of one élite for another. Nevertheless, even in a Britain that continued with its monarchy and aristocracy, greater equalities were eventually won.

People gather every year in Tolpuddle, in the English

county of Dorset, where six agricultural laborers were arrested in 1834 and subsequently deported into hard labor in Australia for trying to form a trade union. The gathering is to celebrate their struggle, suffering and their eventual pardons, won by three years of popular campaigning.

Hundreds and thousands of declarations have been made against tyrants, but the written history of greater equality is largely a bullies' history. Most of what could have been wars of independence were violently put down, with those rising up accused of being rioters or terrorists. The English King, George III, whose actions so incensed those American men, was a classic advocate of inequality. He was very rich but from middle age suffered from recurrent mental and physical illnesses. His granddaughter was Queen Victoria. She was also a great advocate of inequality, opposing rights for women even in the heart of her empire. But the seeds of greater equality were sown under her feet and despite her wishes.

Almost a century after the US Declaration of Independence, back in the heart of the country that had been the primary colonial oppressor and during the height of that reign of Queen Victoria, a much smaller (but in its own way just as great) declaration was made by a woman in a courtroom in London in 1877. Annie Besant stood alongside Charles Bradlaugh. Both were accused of propagating obscenity because, together, they had published a pamphlet on birth control that explained the function of a condom.

A number of eminent Victorians opposed knowledge of contraception becoming more widespread for the reason that it would prevent supposedly brighter people being born as more knowledgeable parents would be more likely to use it. At Annie and Charles' trial, '... some experts, including Charles Darwin, feared that as information became widely available at low cost, it would be used by the wrong sorts of individuals and not by others, so that the salutary effects of natural selection on human perfection would be suspended'.[3]

Besant and Bradlaugh lost the trial and were found guilty of obscenity. What they had done was to make available information that the US birth-control campaigner Charles Knowlton had published 44 years earlier. He had also then been put on trial but the greater equality of rights within the US had still made publication possible.

In hindsight, we know now that, as a result of the Besant-Bradlaugh trial, hundreds of thousands of people in Britain began to use birth control. It was already more commonly used in parts of the European mainland, but contraception quickly spread from Britain to its empire. Population numbers fell rapidly, from almost precisely nine months after the trial, and – as a result – more women had more time to

---

All heroes and heroines of equality are flawed[5]

With the passage of time even the most progressive ideas tend to seem anachronistic. For instance, who do you think are being referred to here? 'They have neither the intelligence, the industry, the moral habits, nor the desire of improvement which are essential to any favorable change in their condition.' The working class? Immigrants? Women? It could be more or less any group as seen by someone with power and privilege but this one happens to be Native Americans, as described by the seventh US President, Andrew Jackson. He went on to say that they were: 'Established in the midst of another and a superior race, and without appreciating the causes of their inferiority or seeking to control them, they must necessarily yield to the force of circumstances and ere long disappear.' He was, sadly, almost right about their disappearing.

Jackson was not unusual in his views. We see similar prejudices at work when the third American President, Thomas Jefferson, wrote in 1853 that he advanced his suspicion 'that the blacks, whether originally a distinct race, or made distinct by time and circumstances, are inferior to the whites in the endowments both of body and mind'. Racist ideas were widespread long before Darwin's '*theory on the origin of species by means of natural selection, or the preservation of favored races in the struggle for life*', had been committed to print.

Annie Besant is perhaps best known for her involvement in the London matchgirls' strike of 1888 where, despite having originally

---

work for greater rights. Annie and Charles were not trying to increase equality in particular, and certainly did not plan to be taken to court and found guilty, but they were moved to act and their acts had huge consequences. Not long after the London trial, fertility also began to fall in India.

The winning of greater equalities can also have unforeseen positive consequences, even when those equalities have been won at the expensive of subordinate groups – and not always because the winners are wonderful advocates of equality. The world does not simply divide into good and evil. Among the Founding Fathers of the US were many racists. *'The American Revolution was carried out in Roman costume, complete with separate assemblies for the élite and the masses (the Senate and the House of Representatives), matching neoclassical*

---

called for a boycott, rather than a strike, she did later work wholeheartedly to help the strikers. But in her old age, Annie Besant took her adopted son from India (where he was born) to the US and proclaimed him the new Messiah. The world is still a better place for Annie, but she was no saint.

Similarly, Richard Tawney, mentioned as an authority on equality in Chapter 2, was often apt to get hold of the wrong end of the stick. He once talked of what he called 'Dr Burt's admirable studies of educational abilities among schoolchildren' which claimed to show that upper-class children were innately more intelligent. Cyril Burt is now known to have forged at least some of his statistics. Richard had been born in Calcutta in 1880 when the British Raj, which ruled over India, was at the height of its power. Growing up in circumstances of great inequality damages anyone's thinking.

Tawney's contemporary, Marie Stopes, argued that the 'sterilization of those totally unfit for parenthood be made an immediate possibility, indeed made compulsory'. And that, if she could, she would 'legislate compulsory sterilization of the insane, feebleminded... revolutionaries... half-castes'. In 1999, she was voted woman of the millennium by readers of Britain's *Guardian* newspaper who cannot have been aware of these particular views. Another even more famous contemporary and hero of radicals, Mohandas Gandhi, is similarly known to have said a few disparaging things about black South Africans. ∎

architecture in the nation's capital, and slaves toiling in the fields'.[4] Today the US is among the more inequitable of affluent nations with a 90:10 income inequality ratio of between 15 and 20, and a fertility rate that exceeds two children per woman.

Over in England, a century after the American Revolution, Annie Besant also held some very odd views (see box above on heroes and heroines of equality). Advocates of inequality, meanwhile, can sometimes spur on equality. If King George III had been a little more reasonable, American independence could have been greatly delayed (and possibly slaves could have been freed earlier in the US). Had Queen Victoria's regime not been so adversarial, there might have been no trial and so no great publicity for Besant and Bradlaugh's leaflet. Hindsight suggests that it is impossible to predict success or failure, but far better to struggle for greater equality than to work on the side that is never later celebrated.

You may think that all the changes described above would have occurred anyway. If it had not been the Founding Fathers, another group of oppressed colonists would have risen up; if it had not been Annie another advocate of birth control would have taken her place... But someone had to take a stand for these things to happen. In Calcutta in 1928, a young barrister who had been trained in London, Mohandas Gandhi, had a resolution adopted at the Indian National Congress calling for complete independence from Britain. Within 20 years it had been won. It need not have been him, but it had to be someone.

When equalities are lost, you have to ask who did not fight hard enough, who did not step forward, or just held their tongue. Later on in this book, examples are shown of how, in specific cases, high levels of equality have been lost. When greater inequalities were advocated and won by small groups in the 1970s in the UK and US, who failed to oppose the changes sufficiently? In India too, why have income inequalities been allowed to grow year on year so that now one per cent of the people receive a tenth of all the country's income, whereas they received less than half that in 1981. The seeds were sown in 'The Emergency' of 1975 to 1977, but why then?

How some rich countries recently set out to become more unequal

Sometimes it actually helps to look at a little data. The graph overleaf shows the percentage of total personal income that goes to the richest one per cent of the population in 12 countries where good data is currently available. The graph shows that it was in 1973 that inequalities in the US reached an all-time low – at this point, the richest one per cent of people earned only 7.7 times the average wage.

Can you imagine a world in which the boss earns just 7.7 times more than the average worker? I grew up in that world. I was 10 years old in Britain when the rich were least rich, when the best-off one per cent earned only 5.7 times the average income. By 2008, that figure had risen to 17.7 times. Almost every year since I was aged 10, I have watched the very rich get richer and, below them, the affluent take more and more of what was left.

Canadians experienced much the same trend, but look again at the graph and you'll see the same was not the case in Germany, or in the Netherlands, or in Sweden, or in France. Not in all rich countries have inequalities risen greatly. In the largest of poorer countries, although inequalities at the very top have risen in recent decades, they are not yet as high as in many of the richest.

The richest one per cent in China still only receive as large an income share there as when the British and Americans were most equal. In India inequalities are greater, but the recent trends have been so similar to

Winning greater equality – and losing it

China and to those seen within much richer countries that it is hard not to believe that something in common is now in play. Other inequalities in those two huge countries are greater. Despite all the hype about their new middle classes, between extreme quintiles of the population, China is as unequal as the US and India even more so.

At the start of the last century, almost everywhere in the world the richest one per cent received between 10 and 20 times average incomes. By 1980, almost nowhere did they receive as much as 10 times the average. Today, at the end of the first decade of another century, although most of the trends have been in the

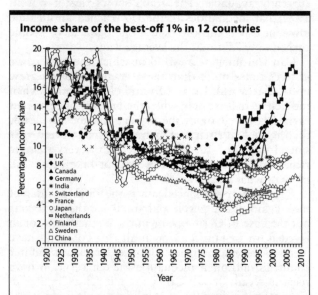

Income share of the best-off 1% in 12 countries

Legend:
- ■ US
- ◆ UK
- ▲ Canada
- ● Germany
- ✻ India
- × Switzerland
- ◆ France
- ○ Japan
- ▦ Netherlands
- ◇ Finland
- △ Sweden
- □ China

Y-axis: Percentage income share

X-axis: Year

Source: The World Top Incomes Database.

wrong direction, we have a wider variety of outcomes between countries in terms of equality and inequality than has ever previously been recorded.

Never before has there been more scope for choice. Never before have the range of inequalities exhibited by these dozen states been as wide as in 2011. Those who wish to see greater equalities won again need to know both how they were lost some 30 to 40 years ago and how in other countries they have been protected. Where inequalities are highest, it is all the harder to recover or improve the situation because: 'Inequality is corrosive. It rots societies from within'.[6]

Here is another way of viewing the trends shown in the graph above. The 12 countries are typical of worldwide trends. For 60 years, inequalities fell rapidly almost everywhere. The income share of the top one per cent in society is just one measure of inequality but it is a good measure in that the use of it ensures that you focus on the rich. In practice, it correlates positively with other measures, but the rich have a disproportionate effect on inequalities given their small numbers. Scholars who study inequality are coming to believe it is very important to concentrate on the rich as the major problem rather than to continue the flawed historical tradition of focusing so much on the poor.[7]

Worldwide, you have to ask how global inequalities might look today had a reformer in the Chinese Communist Party been more concerned about inequalities rising in that country in the 1980s and 1990s. Was the rise in inequalities in China inevitable as it moved towards mass producing the world's merchandise?

How many of the poorest billion people in the world would no longer be poor had more of India taken the path chosen by the citizens of its state of Kerala, which has prioritized health, education and social well-being over decades, with strikingly positive results? Had the industrialist Jehangir Ratanji Dadabhoy Tata not supported the 1975-77 state of emergency in India, would that emergency have survived, would the trend toward growing inequality for a billion people there have become established? And would his steel company now own the forges near where I live in England's former steel capital of Sheffield? There are times when just a single alternative action can make all the difference.[8]

Had 1960s revolutionaries in parts of Latin America been denounced just a fraction less by those who taught the men who went on to run the military regimes of the 1970s, would the world be different? And what might have occurred across Africa, the continent to suffer the greatest falls in income, had people like Tawney just been a little more radical than they were in the 1930s and altered British and other colonialist attitudes just a little bit more? How was the 21-year-old Mohandas Gandhi influenced by the enthusiasm he saw amongst the 3,000 mourners at Charles Bradlaugh's funeral?

To bring this chapter to a close and widen the examples, consider the two largest countries in the world and the long-term view of inequality which can be seen from there. This is done by extracting just two of the lines from the graph on page 74.

For China, the data from this particular set of statistics only begins in the 1980s, but its past patterns of inequality were similar to India's – with the exception that the Communist revolution of 1949 brought Chinese inequalities down much faster and further than in India, though at the cost of great loss of life.

In the years that followed revolution in China, despite famine and hardship, far fewer children died from poverty than in India, not least because fewer were born. Chinese fertility rates came down in a single generation from six live children being born per mother to just over two – and this happened before the introduction of the notorious one-child-per-family policy.[9]

Absolute income equality would see the richest one per cent receive just one per cent of all income (and therefore not be rich). According to this data, China was not far off that point in the mid-1980s (just after its economic boom began), and India was similarly a very equitable (albeit poor) country in so far as it had very few extremely rich people in the early 1980s. In both countries, increased global trading associated with the late-1980s global economic boom, and the acquisition of more of the proceeds of that trading by small affluent groups, resulted in growing inequalities.

From the early 1980s onwards, inequalities in India then soared upwards whereas in China they

Income share of the best-off 1%, India and China

* India
□ China

Note: For China estimates are from urban household income surveys and not from tax data. Also the individual distribution of adult income is shown (data begins 1986).

Source: The World Top Incomes Database.

rose more steadily. Nevertheless, the increase in inequality has not yet brought unfairness in either country back to the levels experienced before 1949 – unlike in the US and the UK, where inequality levels now surpass those earlier highs. And, unlike the first countries to become industrialized, China and India have the errors of the West to learn from – both old errors and very recent ones.

The personal is political

Equality is not an easy subject because it is very personal. The impersonal graphs in this chapter generalize about populations of billions. The richest one per cent shown within the curves of these graphs now number some 70 million people worldwide. Only a very small minority of these are dollar millionaires, and only a tiny fraction of that group are billionaires. In one key aspect the rich, within their own worlds, are as ordinary as everyone else, as all but the very richest have above them a small group of even richer people.

In talking about equality and inequality, we can easily forget greater equality in practice (rather than theory), but it is personal stories that bring home how great historical trends both influence and are made up of billions of tiny actions. In writing this book, I asked a lot of people for help and advice. This is what one wrote:

'I am afraid I struggle with this. I don't feel that I've got a lot of experience of situations where equality prevails and too much of ones where inequality is the norm, and even now, I continually find myself noticing inequalities that should have been bloody obvious, right under my nose. What I can try and talk about is the dramatic impact of those rare people who practice equality – in other words, treat others with the same respect they appreciate themselves, and

whose instinctive reactions to breaches of respect are unimpaired and immediate.

'For example, a teacher I once worked with took on the headship of a really rough primary school in Toxteth [a poorer district of Liverpool] where corporal punishment had been the norm and the previous head had retired after a nervous breakdown. He asked me to come in and help for a couple of days. Somehow, in just one week, he'd transformed the place without ever raising his voice. The kids were still very much themselves: continual, challenging questions and lightning-quick wit; but there was good humor underneath it all. I felt they'd acquired a new self-assurance with Don and found it rather exciting. As I recall, he would call a school meeting if anything interesting (or alarming) happened and just talk with the kids. I got the impression that there was no question he couldn't cope with in an interesting and respectful way, and this was an eye-opener for everyone.'[10]

The overall graph of global inequalities on page 74 can appear very depressing, but in the rest of this *No-Nonsense Guide* it will be taken apart and I will try to show you how your eye has been drawn to the bad news and you are not seeing the good so clearly. The same can happen when you listen to the news on radio or television, which tends to concentrate on disaster and failure.

The countries where inequalities are rapidly rising again have been shaded most darkly, but notice that, in between three-quarters and two-thirds of all the countries included, the best-off one per cent of people still earn less than 10 times average incomes, despite the recent rises in inequality.

Indeed, most of the rich countries of the world still enjoy levels of equality similar to those experienced by Canada, the US and the UK when they were at their most equal. In very special places within unequal affluent countries, and much more widely elsewhere, you can still hear many stories of individuals like Don, who treat other people as equals to amazing effect. But it is far easier to treat others as equals in times and places of greater equality. It is easier to be better when you are all more equal.

1 On the House of Representatives website, see: house.gov/content/learn/history 2 Sebastian Kraemer, personal communication, 2011. 3 See SJ Peart and DM Levy, 'Darwin's unpublished letter at the Bradlaugh-Besant trial: A question of divided expert judgment', *European Journal of Political Economy*, 24, 2008. A free abstract of the piece can be read at: nin.tl/qRMFbq 4 JC Myers, *The Politics of Equality*, Zed Books, London, 2010 5 On Jackson: J Diamond, *The rise and fall of the third chimpanzee*, Random House, London 1992. On Jefferson: WS Shaw, *Cities of Whiteness*, Blackwell, Oxford, 2007. On Besant: nin.tl/nVNPPV On Tawney: A Callinicos, *Equality*, Polity, Cambridge, 2007. On Stopes: nin.tl/pCfnTV and nin.tl/pxOVE3 On Gandhi: nin.tl/rrdoaS 6 T Judt, *Ill fares the land*, Allen Lane, London, 2010. 7 On why it is now worth concentrating on the rich see: Susan George, *Whose crisis, whose future?* Polity, Cambridge, 2010. 8 On the emergency in India and Tata's alleged involvement see: en.wikipedia.org/wiki/The_Emergency_(India) 9 M Connelly, *Fatal Misconception: the struggle to control world population*, Harvard University Press, 2008. 10 Bob Hughes, personal communications, 2010 and 2011.

4 When we were more equal

The history of human equality may surprise you. Hunter-gatherers valued equality and co-operation above all. The happiest and most sustainable societies left no trace, as pyramids and castles are only built by enslaving the poor. Great cultural advances come through revolutions against inequality. Meanwhile, in recent years, English-speaking rich countries have been sending out a warning to the world.

'Geography, sir, is ruinous in its effects on the lower classes. Reading, writing and arithmetic are comparatively safe, but geography invariably leads to revolution.'
1879 testimony before a Select Committee of the House of Commons, London, England, regarding expenditures of the London School Board[1]

WHEN CONSIDERING EQUALITY, it is hard to overstate the importance of humans being mammals. Mammals often live in groups and frequently there are hierarchies to be seen within those groups, from wolf packs to communities of chimpanzees. The key way in which humans differ from other mammals is that they create very elaborate mechanisms to control some people's tendency to try to dominate others. Anthropologist Christopher Boehm described the development of egalitarianism amongst humans as resulting from the *'...collective power of resentful subordinates [which] is the base of human egalitarian society.'*[2] America's Founding Fathers were resentful subordinates.

Hunting, fighting and feasting
Social campaigner Bob Hughes, the man who told us about his friend Don at the end of the last chapter, expounding on Christopher Boehm's work, explains

that a great many of the traits we tend to admire in others today were part of what originally made us human and can today be seen preserved in something possibly similar to their original form:

'Hunter-gatherers, wherever they are found, devote extraordinary care to avoiding the possibility of exciting resentment in others. The greater their personal talents, the more care they take. Accounts of hunter-gatherer societies from all over the world are peppered with vivid examples of the same strong tendency to self-effacement by people who, through their special skills or physical strength, could if they chose try to dominate their peers; and we find an almost identical, well-orchestrated repertoire of techniques deployed against those who show any sign of 'getting above themselves': from gently mocking humor, to gossiping, to ostracism, to abandonment or expulsion and, in the last resort, to homicide. A wise and respected hunter who wants to stay respected makes little of his achievements, and builds his reputation instead on generosity and modesty.'[3]

It is now well established that hunter-gatherer societies relied on relationships of equality and group co-operation to survive. Individuals who acted in selfish ways could be ostracized and would not be likely to survive if they did not find another group.

Fear of being seen as selfish and of being rejected by others is innate in humans who are not psychologically damaged. Christopher Boehm, who is most credited with collating the evidence and articulating these theories, has gone on to suggest that it was partly tool-making that resulted in humans evolving to favor the survival of those among them who were more inclined to be egalitarian. One of Boehm's key explanations as to why our ancestors became more inclined to favor more egalitarian social structures (as compared to the average ape) concerns the advent of a particular group of tools: weapons. Without weapons, the largest and fittest tend to dominate. With weapons, even the smallest can be the killer. Weapons also make it easier for a crowd of smaller humans to dominate a few larger humans, especially when spearheads are attached to long sticks or fired as arrows.

The good news that we evolved to be more equal, and developed ideas of good and evil behavior, is tainted by the bad news that we possibly also symbiotically evolved with weapons and with an innate capacity to work in groups but to kill others if we became frightened enough: *'It is easy, in other words, to prod, push, seduce and entice non-evil people to commit evil things.'*[4]

In detailed analysis of our most recent weapons, it has been very recently suggested that both conventional and nuclear bombs have been used and continue to be readied for deployment not because they serve a military purpose, but because so much money and effort have been invested in creating them.

Zygmunt Bauman, whose words on evil are quoted just above, was writing those words in the context of trying to explain how one German town towards the end of the Second World War was bombed simply because the Allies had run out of other targets and wanted to dispose of some bombs. Thousands of civilians, including many children, were killed.

Part of the reason we do not see war as more repellent is maybe because we have in us both the ability to divide 'us' from 'them' and to be so easily led. However, the creativity that ended up reinforcing those traits could also help us to alter them in future. We are not prisoners of our biology but are far more often locked into ways of thinking that are harmful to all. Often it is only when we have been creative that we have escaped these mental prisons. So far only two nuclear bombs have been dropped to kill.

The greater equality that evolved amongst hunter-gatherers, when unleashed today in situations of respect, leads to greater creativity than is often seen today in unequal societies. Later on in this chapter I list examples of how much more common invention and publishing is in more equitable affluent societies. This is hardly surprising. If you deride a majority of people as being inferior they are unlikely to have the opportunity, let alone the enthusiasm, to create. And creativity is a very old human instinct.

The more tools we made, the more creative we became. The variety became enormous in places such as the floor of the Great Rift Valley, between the two extinct volcanoes of Olorgesailie and Oldonyo Esakut. An opposable thumb was necessary for invention, but it is now widely argued that the greater equality then found between those volcanoes was essential for invention.

Greater equality was also a prerequisite for human settlement. To settle in an area, and especially to farm, requires a degree of co-operation and co-ordination that cannot be sustained easily if the strong are constantly pouncing on the weak. Grasses have to be domesticated. A small surplus needs to be stored to get through the winter, to sow next year's harvest; and, crucially, in case of drought.

However, once settled, a degree of surplus can be amassed that hunter-gatherers would never have been able to amass (let alone carry around with them). If not dissipated, a surplus leads to trouble within any group. It gives the people who hold the surplus power over others which those others may well (and rightly) resent. Mechanisms were developed by imaginative people to prevent the holding of private property destroying many early human societies.

One way to deal with the accumulation of a surplus

is to redistribute it regularly. Potlatch is the name given to those gatherings routinely held around the American Pacific northwest coast to feast, party and redistribute wealth. In fact *'The main purpose of the Potlatch is the redistribution and reciprocity of wealth.'*[5]

In Canada, Potlatch redistribution was made illegal by act of parliament in 1884, the ban only being repealed in 1951. Similarly, in the US, Potlatch was banned *'largely at the urging of missionaries and government agents who considered it "a worse than useless custom" that was seen as wasteful, unproductive, and contrary to "civilized" values.'*[5]

Feasting was developed as a way of redistributing wealth. Celebrations were about coming together. The world's earliest surviving map is of folk dancing in a field – no doubt a more interesting thing to depict than the meal afterwards.[6] But not everywhere did we share.

In some settlements, some people became a little more 'equal' than others. However, the vast majority of early farming does appear to have taken place under quite equitable conditions. Apart from through archaeological records, this is also revealed by many practices still surviving today. It is replacing our own agricultural labor with that of others, and then fewer others and then with machines, that has made much greater inequalities possible.

When inequalities grow, fewer humans grow tall.[7] Human adult skeletons are found to be two to three inches shorter on average if dug up from the places and periods around when hunter-gathering had begun to be given up, and again a further couple of inches shorter from where and when farming became widespread.[8] The reasons suggested for our diminishing heights include not enjoying such a wide variety of nutrients once we became sedentary. We could not (literally) walk away from the problems and places of lean years. But some may also have received less than others when all were not largely collecting for themselves and their wider family.

More of us could live in a smaller area if we farmed; we could preserve knowledge in writing too when slightly larger settlements were established. If we did it sustainably and without creating great hierarchies – and hence differences in who got to eat what – then we would tend to live well but to leave little trace. We have an upside-down view of history where those who create most destruction and carnage, but leave a lot of rubbish and large buildings behind, are remembered (through archaeology) with most awe.

Equitable societies tend not to leave many follies behind. Across most of the continent of Africa, from the more equitable civilizations of the Americas, of Australasia and into Asia and Europe, where people lived well they left the least traces, generally just their bones and a few less perishable essential possessions. A sustainable society leaves as little trace of its existence to be found in the future as is possible. Why would people in an equitable society waste much of their lives building monuments? Monuments are built to demonstrate superiority.[9] And with superiority comes a rationale for conquest. Conquest was then overturned by revolution.

Hierarchy, conquest, revolution

The word 'revolution' is at least seven millennia old. Revolutions have been occurring ever since there has been accumulation of enough power and wealth for it to be worth rebelling over. Without power, it is hard to hold on to wealth and, without wealth, unless you co-operate and share very well, you don't often have much power. It is partly because of wealth that greater equality is so often lost.

The phrase 'revolution' has been dated back to early Egypt. It may be older and may only be dated to then because Egyptian writing is among the earliest that survives. There will have been countless earlier records that have been lost. In ancient Egypt the turn-around of society that resulted from the demoting of a particular Pharaoh was said to be like a *'revolution of the potter's wheel'*.

It is from Egypt that we also have the first recording of an appreciation that all are equally able to contribute and one that even suggests that those who appear to be worth the least and know the least might actually be the wisest. Over 5,000 years ago an Egyptian scribe wrote this saying on papyrus: *'Wise words are rarer than emeralds, yet they come from the mouths of poor slave girls who turn the millstones.'*[10]

Hierarchies arose first in places like Egypt because of geography. It was there that the largest river nearest to the Great Rift Valley entered the sea, shortly after flooding, and hence irrigated the greatest area of surrounding land. If human beings had originated somewhere other than Africa the first great hierarchies would have been found outside Africa. Instead of having African pharaohs immortalized as the first named tyrants of the world, some other group would have been, and their thousands of slaves could similarly now be remembered only as the anonymous tellers of wise truths and turners of millstones, and as the actual unwilling builders of vast monuments.

Our recorded history, especially ancient history, tends to be of non-egalitarian hierarchical societies because more egalitarian non-hierarchical societies had that tendency to blow short-lived surpluses in a Potlatch-type party without leaving many records carved laboriously in stone. When you party more, you leave far fewer monuments behind.

You could not persuade a set of free-minded people to build a pyramid, or for that matter a modern-day cathedral or grand mosque; not for love nor money. You have to enslave the laborers either physically or emotionally to get them to work on huge monuments that serve no obvious utilitarian purpose. Some belief systems make us more free and more equal than others.

It has been suggested that many early religions were partly established in response to growing inequalities and also in order to retaliate against the impact of those inequalities and the frequent enslavement of others that accompanied inequality (see box overleaf). Once the idea of private property is legitimized (ownership of more than a small number of personal items and a patch of land big enough to live on), the idea of property can quickly get out of hand. *Personal* property is limited to what you have about your person. *Private* property is limitless. If anything can be bought and sold, then you can own any amount of land, ideas, incalculable riches, and even other people – slaves.

The Jewish slaves who (among many others) built pyramids had something to hold them together: the idea of an after-life to live for; something invaluable and special to them promised by their one god. The Buddha was a rich aristocrat who gave it all up for something better than material wealth and again that promise of becoming special. The early Christian traditions were all about piety and sharing.

Christians told each other the story of a young rich man who asked Jesus how he could inherit eternal life. Jesus's reply was '...I tell you the truth; it is hard for a rich man to enter the kingdom of heaven. Again I tell you, it is easier for a camel to go through the eye of a needle than for a rich man to enter the kingdom of God.'[11]

Apparently this revelation came as something of a shock to those first Christian disciples, not all of whom were poor. Jesus then is said to have responded: 'If you want to be perfect, go, sell your possessions and give to the poor, and you will have treasure in heaven. Then come, follow me.' It was because the young man had become sad and was unwilling to do this that the eye of the needle was mentioned. The phrase possibly refers to a small gate in a city wall which a camel could fit through only if the saddle and the bags it carried were removed.

It has been claimed that all the great ancient religions began in times of unusually harsh inequality, ranging from conquest, including oppression by a foreign power, to the problems of fair distribution following ecological collapse.[12] Subjugation, inequality and injustice breed dissent and can create new groups who act in solidarity against those who enslave them. The history of Judaism is littered with stories of exodus. In Judea it took the execution of Jesus by the Roman colonizers for Christianity to be born.

Empire and religion

Just as much of our received wisdom on the Egyptians marvels at the splendor of their palaces and the tombs of the few, so the Roman Empire was written up in the textbooks of schoolchildren (in later empires) as being a model of efficiency and order – as something to be emulated. In such schoolbooks the high levels of inequality it fostered, the inefficiency of all roads leading to Rome, of ultimate control by a single emperor, were presented as being for the common good. The US still follows this model with the upper house of Congress named after the Roman Senate and a touching, if unfortunate, belief that a single emperor-president can be infallible.

British Empire era textbooks unwittingly implied the superiority of Roman-style empires, although by then the suggestion was that all roads should lead to London, bringing tribute to the Empress Victoria. This was portrayed as being for the good of almost half of the world, that portion which Britain had colonized. More recently, the US has often tried to dress up its leaders' self-interested action as being for global good. In fact, Roman imperialism did not raise living standards, neither did British imperialism two millennia later, and US imperialism also fails to do so today.

Environmental degradation, religion and equality

Between the first and fourth centuries of the Common Era there was an extended sequence of environmental disasters. These resulted in pestilence and then plague spreading across the Roman Empire. The Roman deities were useful gods for a victorious ruler to believe in, and for a prosperous people to follow, but they were gods of fighting and war. Christianity concentrated on healing and promised a life after death which was of some consolation amid all the excessive dying: 'As conversions to Christianity accelerated during the plagues, it moved from an outlawed religion of martyrs to the official religion of the empire by the end of the fourth century'.[12]

In a similar pattern to when Christianity became widely adopted, the years when Islam came into being, when the Qur'an was first set down and when the prophet Muhammad lived, were also difficult years to live through. The difficulties were partly caused by excessive taxation, but that in turn may have been due to climatic and volcanic precursors which we have only recently come to appreciate. Coping with environmental disasters has often meant having to overthrow long-standing tyranny, and such disasters have often been the trigger that was needed for change to crystallize – to get the established order out of a particular rut of thinking and behaving:

'The decades of fighting which led to the destruction of most of the Arabian kingdoms and chiefdoms seem to have also led to the elaboration of some definite "anti-royal" freedom-loving tribal ethos codified in the tribal historical traditions and poetry... The reflections of this ethos seem to be present even in al-Qur'an [which states... "The kings, when they enter a town, they corrupt it; they make the most glorious of its folk the most base, they do it this way."[13]

During the sixth century, just at the time when the Qur'an was written, there was a global cooling of around 0.7–0.9°C. This was similar to that

Skeletons found recently from times and places of Roman colonization have indicated that people were shorter and in a worse state of health in times of high Roman influence. Far from Roman colonization being a civilizing influence, the damage done to the bones of the skeletons shows evidence of increased disease and starvation. There is even evidence of a curtailing of creativity in the diminishing quality of pottery found in those parts of Europe most colonized by the Romans.

cooling which occurred during the little ice ages of the late 16th and 19th centuries. These all harmed harvests. There was also unusual worldwide tectonic and volcanic activity. It is even claimed that: 'In the history of the Mediterranean region, we may compare it, perhaps, only with the tectonic catastrophe of the middle of the second millennium BCE, which was crowned with the greatest Santorini eruption in the Aegean Sea... that seems to have become fatal for the Minoan Civilization ...'[13] All these events are likely to have harmed harvests, caused widespread fear and made the former tyranny of those kings who entered the towns and corrupted them much harder to maintain than before.

Climatic change and environmental disasters have always had a strong influence on collective human thinking. In Europe, the reaction to the earthquake and tsunami that destroyed Lisbon in 1755 was to crystallize contemporary thinking that there was more to fate than the will of gods. In the world today, enhanced global warming and the perceived threat to planetary ecosystems is again focusing minds in the same way that past events fostered the widespread adoption of new religions, of new ways of thinking. One interpretation of the present is to say that it bears the hallmarks of these past events, and that our paradigmatic beliefs are again being transformed by environmental degradation.

Climatic change has always influenced human society. The advent of ice ages will have coincided with harsher times in more northerly areas and was also the precursor to the invention of agriculture and the transformation of paradigmatic beliefs that often, especially in the cases we can most easily find, entailed the creation of huge monuments. On the subject of such monuments, decaying into dust, the best-known lines may well be Percy Bysshe Shelley's satire on the vanity of inegalitarians: '...on the pedestal these words appear – / My name is Ozymandias, king of kings: / Look on my works, ye Mighty, and despair! / Nothing beside remains. Round the decay / Of that colossal wreck, boundless and bare / The lone and level sands stretch far away.' ∎

Innovation in general stalled in Europe and around the Mediterranean under the yoke of the Roman Empire. Inventions were largely imported from outside rather than created within. More egalitarian China produced a far greater variety of innovations than did subjugated Europe; from the wheelbarrow to (later) printing and gunpowder, from new religious beliefs (the East Asian or Taoic religions) to innovations in both philosophy and ecology.

Across the North China Plain it is said that

a hundred generations of farmers subsisted for centuries without either depleting the soil or needing organization by any all-powerful overlord. Similarly, from India came the third great group of ancient religions, the Eastern or Dharmic religions. Also from India came huge numbers of other ideas, including new languages and mathematics, whose contribution to human history has been played down because it did not suit later European tyrants to admit that not all great ideas were first thought of in Greece. The traditional Western version of history still suggests that innovation and invention rarely occur far from the shores of the Mediterranean and North Seas. These histories tend to start with the Greeks, because earlier European histories did too and because Greece is just within Europe (although it is far from being in Western Europe).

Almost all of the inventions of antiquity originate from times and places where people in general were given more time and space to think – often a long way from Europe. Steel, for instance, had been found in Turkey dating from about 3,800 years ago and from East Africa from three-and-a-half millennia past. Printing, as well as the obvious ceramics, came from China. Spices were cultivated in the East Indies, as – is worth repeating – were many of the ideas that are often today still attributed to Greek philosophers.

The Christian variation on the religious theme of Judaism did result, among much else, in the establishment of monasteries where men were treated as more equal to each other than in the outside world, where learning could be continued, established knowledge protected and new ideas developed. Similarly, the Islamic variation on the Judaic theme resulted in an era of relative peace and quiet trade in goods and ideas in which Indian and Arabian mathematics could mix. For Europeans this thinking later replaced the Roman idiocy of a world in which

CMXLIV represents 944 as 1,000 minus 100 plus 50 minus 10, plus 5 minus 1. There being no 0 in Roman mathematics also limited European intellectual progress.

It was early inequality and tyranny in the Arabian Peninsula, six generations on from tyranny in Judea, which led to the birth of Islam and that early fostering of greater equalities under the new Muslim religion that allowed mathematics to spread westwards. This was preceded by environmental degradation and by a series of outside shocks, similar in psychological impact to how the plague helped usher in Christianity. In the case of Islam it was local groups that helped the new religion spread as they opposed kings trying to collect taxes in lean years.

There is a constant repetition in human history of tyrants emerging and people then banding together to oppose their tyranny. New beliefs and theories are created, new constitutions and creeds constructed, and, then, often that which was created to oppose tyranny and inequality itself becomes corrupted and establishes a new tyranny. In medieval Europe, the Christian Pope became an all-powerful despot. All too often, institutions originally established along egalitarian or emancipatory lines later become purveyors of inequalities and injustice.

The tyranny within Saudi Arabia today, where a tiny royal family controls a huge country; the tyranny of the new Chinese empire that produces mobile flat-screen phones for the social-networkers of the world, using armies of virtual industrial slaves; the tyranny of the terror the US exerts on many smaller states (despite itself having arisen from complaints of such behavior by the British): these are just three of many examples of how the fight for greater equality can be usurped.

The phrase *'all animals are equal but some are more equal than others'* was written by George Orwell in his book *Animal Farm* – a fable about equality and how easily it is lost. It was a parody of the later results of the Russian Revolution. The Tsar of Russia had been a despot. He was overthrown in 1917, only for the revolutionaries that succeeded him in turn to give way to the despots among them. As a result, *'pushed to an extreme never tried anywhere else, the modern promise of bliss guaranteed by a rationally designed and rationally run, orderly society was revealed to be a death sentence on human freedom.'*[4]

Renaissance, mercantilism, enlightenment

Innovation, creativity and greater equality have a long history of being intermingled. Because human beings are so similar in their abilities to each other, under any system based on equal treatment there is a much higher chance of new ideas not only being discovered, but also of those discoveries being recognized as innovative. Under regimes of great inequality, underlings have to tell the emperor how good his fiddling is, even if it is awful and the city happens to be burning down as he plays.

Let us turn our attention now to Europe, near the center of what had been the Roman Empire, but roughly a millennium after it had effectively ceased to exist. The Renaissance in what was later to become Italy was only made possible because of a greater acceptance of more equality.

In 1452 a servant-girl gave birth to an illegitimate boy, Leonardo. He went on to become perhaps the best known painter, sculptor and inventor the world has ever known. Although his achievements are naturally ascribed to his talents, and he has been described as the most talented man to have ever lived, it is also true that he thrived because of when and, more importantly, where he was born. He was born just outside the town of Vinci in the Italian region of Tuscany, whose urban center was Florence.

By the middle of the 15th century, Florence had

The Enlightenment was also one of the first times when the ideas of a named woman were both taken seriously and recorded for posterity. Mary Wollstonecraft's *A Vindication of the Rights of Woman* is, in hindsight, perhaps the most significant thinking to have emerged from the Enlightenment. It was written in 1792, two years after she had written in support of the recent French Revolution, a revolt against both the monarchy and the established church. Mary Wollstonecraft was born just four years after the Lisbon earthquake and died giving birth at the age of 38. Although hardly recognized at the time, and mostly disapproved of when she was discussed, she may have been the most innovative writer of the age.

Communism, colonialism, capitalism

Rebellion often results from finding contemporary inequalities unacceptable, remembering times of greater equality and from the catalyzing effects of natural or human-made disaster. Traditionally, it was the monarch who originally provided a focus for such rebellion. Once kings, queens and emperors are deposed, the next step is the establishment of republics and of greater equality.

Western history marks out the creations of Greek, Venetian, Dutch, French and American republics and, most recently, the creation of an economic union in Europe under no monarch – as moments of great human achievement. These moments are partly remembered in celebration because, following rebellion, the freedom to be more equal can be easily lost again and new tyrannies can very quickly become established in the wake of old. Shortly after celebration, revolution can result in terror, as occurred in France between the summers of 1793 and 1794 (often the terror is the work of counter-revolutionaries). In all of human history, social inequalities rose most abruptly during the 19th century – and most clearly in

grown rich on unequal trade (selling dear and buying cheap) and on a little relaxation of the laws of usury to allow profit to be made from lending money. As yet these riches had not totally corrupted those who received them. Lorenzo de'Medici was the wealthiest of the bankers. However, he took what appeared to be gifted artists and scholars into his household where there '...*was no seating order at table. Instead of the eldest and most respected sitting at the top of the table above the rest, it was the first to arrive who sat with Lorenzo de'Medici, even if he were no more than a young painter's apprentice. And even an ambassador, if he came last, took his place at the foot of the table.*'[10]

Leonardo da (of) Vinci was just one of those young men who came to sit at Lorenzo's table (around 1480). It is ironic that the Renaissance sparked such creativity while also creating a new form of banking, epitomized by the Medicis, which made profit by lending to others and making it permissible to receive interest on those loans.

Most religions had made such moneylending a sin prior to 1480.[14] Islam continues to do so today. However, the moneylending that began in earnest in Florence quickly spread through the mercantilism of the nearby Venetian republic and was imitated more widely. For moneylending to be imitated more widely, a new source of wealth was required. Just a dozen years after Leonardo sat at Lorenzo's table, the ship Santa Maria ran aground on the coast of Hispaniola and the wealth of the Americas became available for plunder.

It was where and when religious rules against profiteering were most weakened that the vicious mercantilism of today began. One of the places made rich by banking, trade and the exploitation of the Americas – and later Africa and the East Indies – was the Dutch Republic (a queendom today). But again, like Florence two centuries before, the Republic was a place that was more welcoming of new thinking than surrounding areas. Now remembered for the Golden Age of Dutch painting, this was also the place where it became possible for René Descartes (1596-1650) to establish a philosophy of science. He would also lament how money appeared to be taking on a life of its own and maddening the minds of people in Amsterdam.

By the 17th century, the Catholic Church, which had once promoted and protected learning, had become far more dominating. Leonardo had been taken to trial for sodomy (and acquitted). The entire republic of Venice had been excommunicated. Galileo (1564-1642), the father of modern observational astronomy, came close to being declared a heretic, and a later pope placed René Descartes' books on the prohibited index, the *Index Librorum Prohibitorum*, in 1663.

Christianity, which had become a very inegalitarian religion, was propping up despotic monarchs, clergy, and stifling all kinds of innovatio within this amoral atmosphere and the added of new-found riches from the New America that modern-day capitalism was born. Ho century on, another external shock, in this Lisbon earthquake and tsunami, would usher equality (see box).

It was Enlightenment thinking that cul in the US Declaration of Independence. It w the Enlightenment that resulted in the efficie a production line version of pin manufactur celebrated in the works of Adam Smith. In th both greater equality and the new human ensla (and greater inequality) of mass factory labor ca of ideas that themselves could only have been sp in a time when we were more equal.

Independent shocks and new thinking in Europe

A relationship of dependence had become established between leaders of both Catholic and Protestant churches, the hereditary aristocracy and particular interpretations of the text of the Bible. This resulted in the proclamation of the supposed divine right of kings to rule – apparently a god-endorsed inequality. In Europe, it took the natural disaster of the 1755 earthquake and tsunami of Lisbon to prompt the questioning of the authority of a god (of any religion) that could sanction such misery. Yet another period of great invention was ushered in under the greater equality that questioning authority allowed. This was freedom from religious dogma and the right to have any thoughts you like (not any amount of wealth). It came to be called the Enlightenment.

'The Enlightenment broke through "the sacred circle" whose dogma had circumscribed thinking. The Sacred Circle is a term used by Peter Gay to describe the interdependent relationship between the hereditary aristocracy, the leaders of the church and the text of the Bible. This interrelationship manifests itself as kings invoking the doctrine of the 'Divine Right of Kings' to rule. Thus church sanctioned the rule of the king and the king defended the church in return.' (From the egalitarian encyclopaedia, Wikipedia).

So, over a thousand years after natural disasters helped bring Islam into existence, the Christian countries themselves had an epiphany. For the tsunami to have had such a great impact on Lisbon, that city itself had to have grown very rich. This had occurred over the previou centuries as gold and silver plundered from the Americas was ported through Portugal and Spain into the rest of Europe and acro India and China.

The so-called 'discovery' of the Americas was akin to a natur aster of epic proportions for the inhabitants of those continent – if they survived the new diseases brought in from the old wor then the social upheaval of, in effect, aliens arriving from what as well have been outer space (the conquistadors) – came to great inequalities, destitution and enslavement. The 'discover fundamentally altered world human geography. In human geo terms it recreated Pangaea (the original landmass in which al nents were joined).

Suddenly Europe took center stage as the crossroads for tra became the place where the Silk Road hit the sea rather than a v peninsula of Asia. In effect, it became a continent despite not b island. The wealth that amassed in Europe as a result of trans- exploitation was one of the catalysts for later social change b dramatic, but it took that 1755 environmental disaster finally beliefs away from the view that god approved of inequality and gave kings divine rights. Some 34 years after the Lisbon eart revolution took place in France. Environmental and social ev always far from unrelated.[15] ∎

those parts of the world which were industrializing. Before industrialization, fashions changed slowly and the consumption of material goods was low. There were limits to both growth and to the wealth that could be accumulated when people relied on the sun, wind and water as their primary means of power.

Before industrialization, people were not necessarily poor. If they survived childhood disease they could live very good lives, often working far fewer hours a day than their descendants laboring in factories or offices, but they had much less stuff. The richest amongst them especially had less. Today in rich nations, it is often remarked that even some of the poorest among us can have access to goods and a degree of comfort not even enjoyed by kings in the recent past; the poor can have lots of stuff, but often are not respected.

It was when the more natural and sustainable power sources were replaced by burning coal that so much extra stuff could first be made. Steam was generated to drive machines which could more quickly transform one commodity into another: wool into jackets, iron into nails. But the machines could not run themselves. There was suddenly, it appeared, no limit to what could be accumulated by a small group of people who enslaved others to work for them, magnifying the effects of that labor by attaching human beings to looms and other machines. Wage slaves might appear to be politically free, but have no real choice over the work they have to do.

The first of the extra stuff that was produced by these wage slaves might have appeared to be necessities. Cotton garments were manufactured in huge quantities. A great proportion of the world's people became clothed in garments manufactured in England. The wage slavery in England and Scotland was not the only thing that made this possible. It also occurred because actual slaves taken from Africa had been put to work in American plantations to pick that cotton – and because the clothing industry across the whole Indian subcontinent was repeatedly and ruthlessly decimated. Inequalities were raised, both worldwide and within the newly industrializing countries. Within Britain, as little of the surplus as possible was passed on to the mill workers.

It was out of this new, steep rise in inequality that communism was born. Karl Marx was simply the person who was there at the time and who most effectively addressed the rising inequality he saw around him. He had a ready audience as far more people than he and his colleague Friedrich Engels could see that inequalities were rapidly rising. Marx was the author of the most cogent analysis of the time, *Das Kapital*, and also co-author (along with Engels) of *The Communist Manifesto*.

It was the capacity of coal-burning to power machines and make huge profit that made the times new – that provided the environmental 'shock'. The *'…initial fears centered on the possibility that the benefits of this new capacity would be confined to a tiny minority. Das Kapital embodied this fear and encapsulated the anger which moved millions in much of the 20th century'*.[16] Marx thought Russia almost the last place on earth likely to take up his suggestions, but it was Russians in exile planning a revolution who found his ideas to be the best then on offer.

Although he could not have known it, Karl Marx was writing at a time and in a place (Victorian England) of extremely, if not unprecedentedly, high inequality. By the 1850s in England, people's average heights were at an all-time low. They recovered only slowly. By 1918, average heights were only back to where they had been a century earlier in 1818.[17]

Life expectancy in the worst parts of Manchester and Glasgow could be as low as 25 for decade after decade in the early 19th century, and this was from within the powerhouses of the country at the center of the British Empire. Overall life expectancy was so low because so many infants died. Childhood diseases spread easily in dense, poverty-wracked slums.

The global impoverishment that the spread of capitalism would bring – at first out of Amsterdam, then out of London and finally centered on New York – would result in the worldwide stunting of millions of children as imperialism brought recurrent famines to the India of the British Raj and (opium) war to China.

Many Indians fought for and gained independence (followed by terror and mass exodus as Pakistan separated). Many Chinese fought for and gained a revolution – again one that was followed by terror. However, it was the 1917 revolution in Russia that had the greatest effect worldwide.

The Russian revolution caused great fear among some of the most powerful people in the richest countries of the world. Suddenly it looked as if revolution was possible even in the most backward of places. For Britain, internal revolution was simultaneously occurring within what was to become the Republic of Ireland, which had been part of the United Kingdom but saw the Easter Rising of 1916 lead ultimately to independence in 1922.

The graph overleaf shows just the French and UK shares of income from that complex more complete graph introduced early on in this guide. The French records are more complete. However, prior to 1950, other records showed the British had a similar experience to the French: one of rapidly growing equality from the mid 1920s to the mid 1970s. The latest figure for the UK in the graph is taken from 2005. Since then, the best-off one per cent have seen their share of incomes rise even faster while most British people's real incomes have fallen.

The British loss of most of Ireland; fear of revolution in England; the aftermath of the First World War; the rise in progressive leftwing parties; strengthening trade

When we were more equal

unions; the first wave of feminism; the beginnings of various civil-rights movements: all of these led to slight decreases in the share of national income received each year by the very rich.

Why did inequality fall in places like Britain and France from 1920 onwards? One suggestion is that immediately after the First World War many poor countries were carved up and divided amongst the victors. The profits from colonial spoils enjoyed by the victors were just another reason why it became possible to reduce inequalities within these rich countries.

Inequalities fell within rich countries like the UK

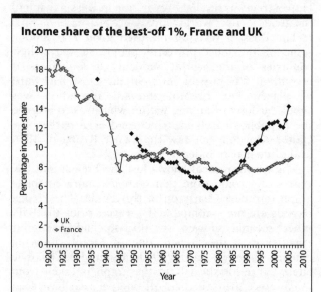

Income share of the best-off 1%, France and UK

Note: For the UK, until 1974, the estimates relate to income net of certain deductions; from 1975, estimates relate to total income. Until 1989 estimates relate to tax units but, from 1990, estimates relate to adults. Data for the UK is patchy prior to 1951.

Source: The World Top Incomes Database.

and France between 1920 and 1970 partly because they were rising worldwide between countries. While inequalities were growing worldwide, and local traditional industries in poorer countries were being decimated by the demand for free trade from rich countries, within rich countries new equalities were being won.

The great period of growing equality in both the UK and France (and in many other affluent nations, but not Germany) was between the two world wars, and it continued right through into the 1970s. This is seen in many monetary and physical measures. For instance, children's heights soared upwards in most affluent countries where equalities increased.

There was also a great fear of communism, which was heightened from the 1920s onwards as it became clear the Russian revolution was not about to be reversed. The 1929 banking crash appeared to be Marx's predicted collapse of capitalism. Labor movements grew stronger. Even in the 1960s, many thought that communist countries were more efficient, able to get astronauts into space first. It wasn't until the 1980s that, excepting China, they were seen as economic basket cases.

Paul Krugman, in his book *The Conscience of a Liberal*, suggests that all the main changes in US inequality that occurred throughout the 20th century were driven by politics. Initially that politics resulted in much greater economic equality being achieved within the US than was experienced in much of Europe. Ordinary people in the US had a high standard of living by the 1960s.

By the 1970s, some of the tallest people on earth were those who were born in the US. Inequalities were at an all-time low, unprecedented numbers of young people were allowed to go to college and university for the first time, and civil rights were being won by both black groups and women. Technological innovation permitted white American men to demonstrate that they could travel on a rocket to the moon and get back alive – though, in hindsight, the refusal of Rosa Parks to give up her seat on an Alabama bus in 1955 had more long-term effect.

A kind of second American revolution took place between 1928, when the richest one per cent of Americans took almost a fifth of all national income, and 1973, when that share had fallen to just 7.7 per cent, the lowest ever recorded (see graph below). Women, people from minority ethnic groups, youngsters – and, above all, poorer people – secured greater equality in the US than had existed since the time when indigenous peoples dominated the land.

Social democracy versus corporate greed

In 1905 the US Supreme Court declared as unconstitutional a new law that had been introduced in New York State. This law limited the working hours of a baker to 10 per day. The Court said this *'deprived the baker of the liberty of working as long as he wished'*.[18] The average working week then in the US was 60 hours.

In 1905, and for much of the 30 years that followed, the richest one per cent of US citizens managed to take home up to a fifth of all the national income each year – as much as 20 times the average worker's earnings (taking the arithmetic mean) and much more than that if you took the median income (median income is that amount at which half the working population earns less and half more).

A century ago, in England, two out of every five women in work were domestic servants.[19] They might well be working 60 hours or more a week. Most of the remaining female employees worked in factories and mills, where at least their working hours were limited to 56 a week by the Factory Act of 1878. But on the whole the period was one of dog-eat-dog. Regulations were seen as evil and if a baker wished to work himself to an early death, but undercut his competitors by so doing (hence also hastening their deaths through overwork), then so be it.

'Less regulation' was the wish of many in power, but others successfully opposed the powerful. It was in response to such opposition that Britain had brought in that 1878 Factory Act and that New York State later introduced that 1905 law. And because those who opposed became better organized, greater equalities were permitted and enforced, fought over for three decades and then reinforced for four decades more.

If just the Canadian and US lines are shown on the graph of the shares of income held by the best-off one

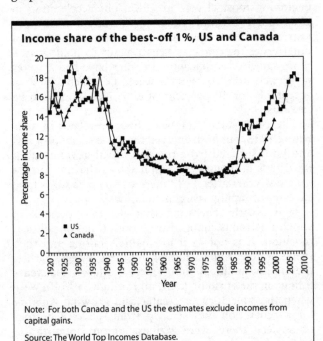

Income share of the best-off 1%, US and Canada

Note: For both Canada and the US the estimates exclude incomes from capital gains.

Source: The World Top Incomes Database.

per cent, then the achievements of the 1930s become clearer to see. It is also evident that, prior to the late 1930s, these two countries were similar but followed differing trajectories. From the middle of that decade onwards they tracked each other downwards – rapidly – as the outcome of the 1929 stock-market crash and the mass unemployment that followed it eventually led to the rich being denied such an unfair share. They continued to be denied it until most adults alive in the 1930s were dead or were too old to be taken sufficiently seriously when they warned us of the folly of allowing inequalities to rise so high again.

Inequalities rose in the 1980s almost as fast as they had fallen in the 1930s. The increases were abrupt, beginning most clearly in 1982, but accelerating in 1986 and 1987, and rising significantly almost every year since. They rose as North American ideas of unfettering the markets began again to hold sway – those same ideas that would earlier have had a baker work well over 60 hours a week, or which saw it as acceptable for 40 per cent of employed women to be servants.

The two North American lines were not in sync before 1938, but both enjoyed the same social progress and both suffered from the anti-social 'revolution' of the 1980s (although the graph shows that in Canada for a few years after 1989 there was a curtailing of the excesses of rapidly rising inequalities).

It is worth reiterating that the two periods in which the trends changed were both times of political rebellion. It is not as if inequalities falling and then rising follow some kind of business cycles; rather, they follow political victories and failures. The years following the crash of 1929, all through to 1940, were when the trajectory of greater and growing equality for a generation was set. Up from the very bottom of society there were strikes, union organization and early civil-rights agitation. Down from the top came fear of revolution and rebellion. Within the Democratic Party in the US, a mood for change was successfully established, a new deal and social state offered, defended and extended through the 1950s and 1960s.

Just as the ownership and profit from colonies made growing equalities in Europe cheaper for European élites, greater equality in the US and Canada was partly made possible by North America's increasing dominance of international markets. As North American riches grew greatly, sharing the surplus became easier than would otherwise have been the case and than was the case in the 1930s depression. This was because so often the greater sharing out in the US and Canada was at the expense of peoples elsewhere in the world, people who were having free trade imposed upon them in a singularly unfree way. North American soldiers were fighting a great many hot wars and a gigantic Cold War, mostly to pursue their selfish economic interests.

The second period in which the trends changed was from 1968 to 1980. By the end of these years, rightwing politics had won pre-eminence and the Republican Ronald Reagan came to power as US president. Near the start of these years President Nixon, also a Republican, had ended the international system of financial exchange, so that he no longer had to guarantee a dollar was worth a certain amount of gold. It was by these years also that most colonies had formally gained independence, that the oil-producing countries became more independent, that industrialization spread, and that the balance of world economic power began to alter.

Human discovery of the uses to which coal and oil could be put are very closely intertwined with falls and rises in equality – both those inequalities that began growing when coal-powered industrialization took shape and those that grew as cheap oil became scarce towards the end of this second period. Richard Nixon floated the dollar free partly so as to allow the US to buy more of its oil from abroad. Floating the dollar free also allowed Nixon to finance a particularly nasty war, in Vietnam.

All of this had to be done because the US was no longer becoming richer and richer in comparison to the rest of the world, as it had in the post-World War Two years when economic growth had been unprecedented (possible only because Europe was war-ravaged). Continued economic growth at post-War US rates was unsustainable and, from 1980 onwards, it looked as if living standards in North America could not continue to rise so quickly.

The next North American revolution was organized by the most affluent, who had become used to great rises in living standards year after year. They did not realize that these had not arisen solely (or even largely) because of the ingenuity of Americans, but mostly because of the effective exploitation of others. US far-right advocates, such as George Gilder, rose to prominence in the early years of Ronald Reagan. His *'four word answer to poverty was "Get married, stay married" and that marriages break down "because the benefit levels destroy the father's key role and authority"'.*[20]

In 1987, the American Enterprise Institute for Public Policy Research working seminar issued the following statement: *'"The way to move out of poverty is to finish high school, get married and stay married, and take (and keep) a job." This has been the neoliberal consensus on " poverty policy" ever since.'*[20]

Today in the US, austerity measures are presented as being the only permissible policy discourse, even though academics write that one cause of the deficit is non-progressive taxation and conclude that *'inequality is not only unethical but also it is economically disastrous'.*[21]

Very recently, public-sector cuts, especially when

accompanied by regressive taxation (the rich pay less), have been shown by economists to be statistically linked to rioting and violence. This relationship is so close that those finding it even suggest that this is one mechanism that prevents unjust governments from increasing inequalities even further. Thus *'one possible reason why austerity measures are often avoided –[is] fear of instability and unrest'*.[22]

For those of us unfortunate enough to live in inequitable countries, but fortunate enough to live in the rich world, we have to look back to before the 1980s to recognize the great equalities that were lost, to see other possibilities in practice where we live. We have to work hard to remember what it was like to live in the US when Americans were more equal. When they were more equal, more found it easier to stay married to someone they loved, to find a job they liked and to stay longer at school than their parents. It was similar in Britain, but Britain is now almost as unequal as the US and, during 2011-15, will undergo £81 billion ($130 billion) of public-sector cuts which will be mostly to the detriment of those with less.

In Britain, the Conservative-led coalition government of 2010 slashed the public debt, sought to curb inflation, drove down wages and tried to take control of the trade unions. When social inequalities had been as high before in Britain, the British élite chose in the end not to follow others in Europe when *'Benito Mussolini and Hitler had slashed the public debt, curbed inflation, driven down wages, and taken control of the trade unions in Italy and Germany, respectively.'*[23] They might still not follow through on that route, but the signs as I write this are not good. A December 2010 government report misleadingly titled 'Tackling child poverty and improving life chances, consulting on a new approach' argued that *'We are particularly concerned about evidence demonstrating that poverty is transmitted between generations'* and 'The evidence available indicates that simply increasing household income, though reducing income poverty, will not make a big difference to children's life chances.'[24] That is simply wrong.

This concentration on anglophone affluent countries is necessary because they now serve as a warning to so much of the world. In the UK and the US there has been a revival of 1960s Cultural Deficit Theory – the discredited idea that underachievement among poor children was a result of deficiencies within the children, their families and communities.[25]

The cultural deficit models argued that, since poor parents failed to embrace the educational values of the dominant social classes, and continued to transmit to their children values which inhibited educational achievement, then the parents' culture was to blame if low educational attainment continued into succeeding generations.

Reviving discredited ideas allows extremist governments to recommend measures which then entirely ignore the structural reasons for educational underachievement, reasons such as inadequate school funding in poor areas, social class segregation in the education system, low-quality teaching, thousands of children being excluded from school, schools' failure to prevent bullying, teacher prejudice against certain children and so on and on.

Within the US today, wealth inequalities have recently risen rapidly as measured between households designated ethnically white and those labeled black or Hispanic. This increase in inequality in wealth began before the economic crash of 2008, but was greatly exacerbated by it. The first of the two charts opposite shows that, by 2009, the average black family had recourse to 19 times less wealth than the average white family.

When all the wealth of black households in the US is averaged out, by 2009 there was just $5,677 to share out among every household. Just four years earlier

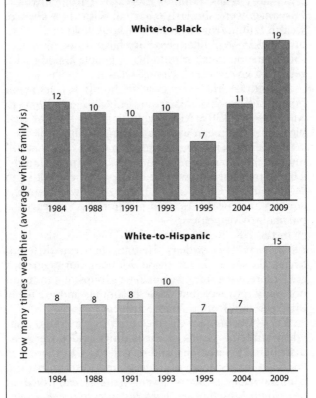

Change in wealth inequality by ethnicity in the US

White-to-Black

How many times wealthier (average white family is)

1984	1988	1991	1993	1995	2004	2009
12	10	10	10	7	11	19

White-to-Hispanic

1984	1988	1991	1993	1995	2004	2009
8	8	8	10	7	7	15

Notes: The survey of Income and Program Participation was redesigned for the 1996 panel. The redesign may have affected the comparability of the data from 1998 and later years with the data from earlier panels.

Sources: For 2009: Pew Research Center tabulations of Survey of Income and Program Participation data from the 2008 panel; for 1984 to 2004: various US Census Bureau Reports including *Current Population Reports*.

that figure had been $12,124. The housing-market crash hurt black families especially hard. However, Hispanics were similarly affected, with their average wealth falling from $18,359 per household in 2005 to just $6,325 by 2009. These are huge drops over very short time periods for millions of people already with relatively low levels of average wealth.

In contrast, the average white family saw its mean household wealth fall from $134,992 in 2005 to $113,149 by 2009. Most white families are not that wealthy – the mean average is dragged upwards by a very rich minority – but the median white family is still much richer than the median black or Hispanic family. The figure above shows just how great the wealth gap by race in the US now is.[26] Having low wealth in the country that perceives itself as the richest on earth is particularly demeaning.

In the UK, meanwhile, inequalities have also been rising fast. This widens the gaps between different social classes and, for those ethnic-minority groups over-represented in lower-income groups, it can mean not only poverty but also becoming more visibly differentiated from the more affluent majority.[27]

A 2011 summary of recent evidence found that when studying issues of inequalities and poverty as distributed by ethnicity and race in the UK, there was common experience of racism and discrimination. *'But as soon as nearly every issue is examined in more detail, such broad patterns start to break down. Discussing issues in relation to "minority ethnic groups" as a whole almost immediately becomes untenable due to the enormous variation between them. Even considering a smaller set of ethnic groups is very often also problematic... For other "groups", such as Chinese people, the variations of income as well as many other factors are so wide as to bring into question when it is useful to use this single group as a focus for analysis.'*[28]

Today, 90 per cent of world wealth is held by just 1 per cent of the world's human inhabitants. Inequalities between countries are falling slightly as they rise rapidly within them, so all of us *'feel insecure because our jobs, and so our incomes, social standing and dignity, are under threat...'* The result is that *'the explosive compound of growing social inequality and the rising volume of human suffering, relegated to the status of "collaterality" (marginality, externality, disposability, not a legitimate part of the political agenda) has all the markings of being potentially the most disastrous among the many problems humanity may be forced to confront, deal with and resolve in the current century.'*[4]

1 Mark Lawrence, Geography Dept, Bemidji State University, Minnesota, US. nin.tl/nPS1eK 2 Christopher Boehm, *Hierarchy in the Forest: The Evolution of Egalitarian Behavior*, Harvard University Press, 1999. 3 Bob Hughes (forthcoming), *The Socialist Computer: life, work and technology among equals*, Pluto, London. On Bob's campaigning see dustormagic.net 4 Zygmunt Bauman, *Collateral Damage*, Polity, Cambridge, 2011. 5 nin.tl/o6Nqrw, referring to GM Sproat, quoted in D Cole and I Chaikin, *An Iron Hand upon the People* (Vancouver/Toronto 1990). Potlatch is common all around the Pacific but varies in how it is described. In New Zealand/Aotearoa the term is Hāngi. 6 It is a map because it is thought to show the field boundaries around the dancers. Maps were drawn long before there was writing. A very concise history of cartography is given in D Dorling and D Fairbairn, *Mapping, ways of representing the world*, Longman, London, 1997. 7 Very recent work is beginning to show that the Roman invasion reduced the heights attained by those invaded. Advocates of inequality often claim it allows 'Tall Poppies' to grow without realizing that they can only look tall because it stunts the growth of so many around the few. 8 S Wells, *Pandora's Seed: The unforeseen cost of civilization*, Allen Lane, London, 2010. Women up to 9,000 BCE stood on average 5.6 inches above five feet in height. That fell to 1.2 inches above by 5,000 BCE and 0.7 inches by 3,000 BCE. For men, the drop was from 8.7 to 6.8 to 3.5 inches in those 6,000 years. 9 Numerous theories abound over men in particular needing to prove something, most recently by building tall phallic skyscrapers, earlier by having constructed great womb-like halls (the womb being the most powerful muscle in the human body). The psychology of inequality and equality is almost limitless, but it can be worth starting with issues of masculinity: S Kraemer, 'The Fragile Male', BMJ 321:1609-12, 2000. 10 EH Gombrich, *A Little History of the World*, New Haven, Yale University Press, 2008. 11 On the rich, needles and camels: nin.tl/nMcMMp 12 WF Ruddiman, *Plows, plagues, and petroleum*, Princeton University Press, 2005. 13 A Korotayev, V Klimenko and D Proussakov, 'Origins of Islam: Political-Anthropological and Environmental Context', *Acta Orientalia*

When we were more equal

Academiae Scientiarum Hung 52(3-4): 243-276, 1999. **14** The inner ring of the seventh circle of hell was reserved for those lending money according to one 14th-century interpretation of Christianity, Dantë's *Divine Comedy*. See: nin.tl/r2qlus **15** A summary of suggestions in Peter Gay, *The Enlightenment: An Interpretation*, W W Norton, 1996, and Wikipedia which, by July 2011, had been edited by 16 people: en.wikipedia.org/wiki/Age_of_Enlightenment. In 2002 and 2005 Susan Neiman and Jean-Pierre Dupuy also separately identified 1755 as the date after which we saw that we could overcome natural disasters if we organized ourselves better. **16** EA Wrigley, *Energy and the English Industrial Revolution*, Cambridge University Press, 2010. **17** R Floud, K Wachter et al, *Height, health and history: nutritional status in the UK, 1750-1980*, Cambridge University Press, 1990. **18** HJ Chang, *23 things they didn't tell you about capitalism*, Allen Lane, London, 2010. **19** S Robson & M McGuinness, 'Gender inequality and women's poverty', in B Knight, *A minority view: What Beatrice Webb would say now*, Alliance Publishing Trust, London, 2011. **20** David Gordon, personal communication, 2011. **21** R Peet, 'Inequality, crisis and austerity in finance capitalism', *Cambridge Journal of Regions, Economy and Society* doi:10.1093/cjres/rsr025, 2011. **22** J Ponticelli & HJ Voth, *Austerity and Anarchy*, Centre for Economic Policy Research, London, 2011. Open access copy at: nin.tl/qv7wzQ **23** J Bakan, *The Corporation*, Constable, London, 2005. **24** The original, as of Nov 2011, could be found on the web here: nin.tl/vo6inZ **25** Discredited by, among hundreds of others, D Gordon, in G Craig, T Burchardt and D Gordon, *Social Justice and Public Policy*, Policy Press, Bristol, 2008. **26** Rakesh Kochhar, Richard Fry and Paul Taylor, 2011, nin.tl/oDlVYp **27** See D Dorling, *Fair Play: Selected Readings on Social Justice*, Policy Press, Bristol, 2011. **28** Joseph Rowntree Foundation, 2011 nin.tl/q24tqs

5 Where equality can be found

It is fair to say that heaven on earth has not been achieved yet, nor will it be soon. But it is perfectly possible to identify countries that are already benefiting from higher levels of equality and to try to learn from their example. Just as important is to identify the most inequitable countries so as to avoid taking their road.

'A map of the world that does not include Utopia is not worth even glancing at, for it leaves out the one country at which Humanity is always landing.

'And when Humanity lands there, it looks out, and seeing a better country, sets sail. Progress is the realization of Utopias.'

Oscar Wilde, 1891

EQUALITY IS LOOKING forward to the weekend. It is during the weekend that you are free to choose how to use your time and are most equal to others – and so have the fairest set of choices.[1] During the week you are told where to sit in school or which lectures to attend or you have to obey your employer or desperately search for work or justify not being in paid labor (unless you are deemed too old or sick to work). Equality matters because it is freedom. The story of the weekend is one of a million stories of more equality being better than less.

Just as there are times in the past, and even two days every week, when equality tends to have been greater, so too there are places near to you now where it is greater than where you are, and places further away. There are even places now where people live lives that are more similar to those around them than ever before in written history. None of these places are utopia, but they are places from which it is at times easier to look towards where utopia lies. In many places terrible events occur, freedoms are impinged and poverty continues to damage lives; and yet they still point towards a better future and away from a worse and even more inequitable past.

It is usually in comparison to other nearby countries, or to areas of similar wealth (but not similar equality) that places of greater equity look good. Compared to Haiti, which is the most inequitable of Caribbean nations, Cuba (the most equitable) looks great. Compared to what you might wish heaven on earth to be like, Cuba remains a long way from it. This chapter begins with Cuba and ends with hopes and dreams.

Cuba, Costa Rica and Kerala

Cuba has two secret weapons. First, the state tries to reduce the gap between rich and poor. Like any state, this does not include the favored bureaucrats, who still benefit from being bureaucrats, but not by as much as bureaucrats in rich unequal countries appear to benefit. Second, there is community self-support and care at local levels, which has arisen as a response to the more regressive aspects of the state, but which actually also reinforces its redistributive elements. Cuba shows you need a state to provide the necessary conditions, and you need sufficiently strong communities to take these forward.

Cuba stands out in international comparisons as a result of meeting both the necessary and sufficient conditions despite the decline of the Soviet Union, its former sponsor. In 2010, Cuban life expectancy at 79 years exceeded that in many US states as well as that in Barbados (78), the Czech Republic (77), Poland (76), Slovakia (75) and, nearer to home, the very affluent but very inequitable Bahamas (74).

Five more years of life expectancy in Cuba, as compared to the Bahamas, is 55 million more years of living and breathing for today's 11 million Cubans. The Gross National Income per person in the Bahamas is over $25,000 per person. In Cuba it is $5,500, less than a quarter as much money. Thus, despite poverty, Cubans each live on average five years longer.[2] If a country as poor as Cuba can achieve all this, then what more would be possible if greater equality were achieved in more affluent nations?

In Cuba, the average adult has benefited from 10.2 years of schooling. That is more than in Luxembourg (10.1), Hong Kong (10.0), and the Mediterranean islands of Malta and Cyprus (both 9.9). It is also more than in: Austria (9.8), Italy (9.7), Peru (9.6), Malaysia (9.5), and a lot more than in the United Kingdom (9.4).[3] The United Kingdom scores so low because it was so very élitist in its recent past when most children were consigned to inferior secondary modern schools or, before that, to no secondary education at all.

The United Nations calculates an 'expected years of schooling measure', which is the number of years of schooling that a child of school entrance-age can expect to receive if prevailing patterns of age-specific enrollment rates were to stay the same throughout the child's lifetime. That figure for the UK in 2010 was 15.9 years, but for Cuba it stands at 17.7 years.

Only four countries in the world can better what a Cuban child might expect in terms of UN-predicted future years of education: Australia (20.5 years), New Zealand/Aotearoa (19.7 years), Iceland (18.2 years) and Ireland (17.9 years). These last two may have trouble maintaining those records due to recent economic shocks – shocks to which Cuba is now far more resilient, having survived the demise of the Soviet Union.

More equitable countries tend to favor educating everyone for longer. The four countries immediately below Cuba in the 2010 ranking were: Norway (17.3), Finland (17.1), Denmark (16.9) and the Republic of Korea (16.8 years). In contrast, Canada sits lower, alongside the UK, but at least both of those are above the US (15.7 years).

Where equality can be found

There are currently around two million children in Cuba aged under 15. That is an extra four million years of education they can currently expect to receive as compared with a similar number of children living in the US, or just over a year each of those extra five years they can expect to live being spent in *extra* education, as compared with the apparently more affluent citizens of the Bahamas.

How can levels of health and education be so much better in Cuba than in other more affluent nations? The simple answer is that how healthy the population is and how much they all know is taken much more seriously in countries where other human beings are considered as being more equal in value. Many complain that in Cuba civil liberties are curtailed and it is certainly possible to imagine Cuba becoming a much better country than it is. But it is also even more easily possible to imagine all those richer countries which score so much worse than Cuba in terms of health and education doing much better too, if only they would learn to become a little more equal.

Costa Rica sits not too far from Cuba and is another nation-state often presented as a role model for the benefits of greater equality. Given that it has not had to suffer under a US embargo or to recover from the collapse of the Soviet Union, Costa Rica is a richer country than Cuba. However, income is a little less equitably distributed in Costa Rica than in Cuba. As a probable consequence, despite having twice the per-capita income, it has only a similar life expectancy to Cuba. Maternal mortality is lower in Costa Rica, but years spent in education are also lower. Women hold 37 per cent of parliamentary seats in Costa Rica, but in Cuba women are nearer to achieving parity, with 43 per cent of all seats. Both these proportions are far greater than those most rich countries achieve.

Before quibbling about different models and levels of greater equality, compare the statistics for both

Costa Rica and Cuba with the latest for nearby Haiti, which is both incredibly poor and incredibly unequal. In Haiti, life expectancy had fallen to 61.7 years even before the 2010 earthquake; mean average years in education were down to 4.9; expected years to 6.8; maternal mortality was 22 times more frequent than in Costa Rica; and, perhaps unsurprisingly, women in parliament made up only five per cent of all parliamentarians.

More equitable countries deal far better with natural disasters than do more inequitable countries. In fact, most of the effect of a natural disaster is not natural but is influenced by the nature of the society that is hit. When earthquakes hit Haiti or hurricanes hit the US, the effects are far worse than they are in more equitable countries that experience similar disasters, because so many more people are so much poorer in more unequal nations.

Cuba and Costa Rica differ in many ways but they are similar in two key respects. First, they are more equitable countries compared with those next door (Nicaragua and Panama in Costa Rica's case, every other Caribbean island in Cuba's). Second, they have resisted colonial and US interference, unlike Haiti.

In Haiti, revolution followed slave rebellion in 1791 but former slave owners were replaced by new élites made up of the better-off ex-slaves. In contrast, the Cuban revolution came much later (1953-9). Costa Rica, located much further to the west, resisted enslavement by the original Spanish colonizers more effectively. The death penalty was abolished in Costa Rica as early as 1877, at a point when Cuba was still a Spanish colony and when the Haitians were still paying reparations to France for their freedom.[4]

Costa Rica severed diplomatic relations with Cuba in 1961 and only reinstated them in 2009. Not all places on the road to utopia are well connected. The government in Costa Rica was also initially hostile to

Nicaragua when revolution was taking place there in the early 1980s, but later the Costa Rican president helped negotiate the 1987 peace plan whereby the US promised to stop funding insurrection in Nicaragua. All this was done without his country having any armed forces. Costa Rica is the most celebrated of about two dozen of the world's countries that have chosen to have no army, navy or air force.

Finally, what of Kerala, the third place in the title of this section? You don't hear much about Kerala because it is not a country. It is a state of India, much larger in area and population than most countries, but not a nation-state.

If Kerala were a country it would be with this little group of three places signposting routes to utopia. Its life expectancy is 75 years for men, 78 years for women and its literacy rate is unsurpassed in all of India, at over 95 per cent.

In 2005, Kerala was acknowledged as having one of the highest rates of human development in the world and *'after 10 years of secondary schooling, students typically enroll in Higher Secondary Schooling in one of the three major streams – liberal arts, commerce or science.'*[5]

Kerala is not a rich Indian state, but it is an equitable one. In the 1991, 2001 and 2011 censuses, the sex ratios of women to men rose from there being 3.6 per cent more women, to 5.8 per cent, to 8.4 per cent more.[6] Across much of the rest of Asia and almost all of India there are more men than women because female fetuses are selectively aborted, young girls are less well cared for and die in childhood, more young women die in child birth, and elderly women are also less well cared for. Kerala shows how different things can be.

Kerala is known outside of India often for being one of the states where the communist party does well in elections. However, its lack of beggars due to greater equality (despite incomes not being especially high) may be just as much a product of other factors – its outward-looking cultural traditions; its efficient use of international trade and remittances; its centuries-old religious tolerance, including a long-established Jewish population; the mountains and jungle that cut it off from much of the rest of India – as it is a product of its more radical politics and the higher status accorded to women than is usual in the subcontinent.

Norway, Sweden and Finland

If Cuba, Costa Rica and Kerala show what is possible in some of the poorer countries and states worldwide then the three main Scandinavian countries show what can occur when greater equality is mixed with great affluence. In Norway, the amount of wealth generated through extracting oil has been huge, but rather than use it to enrich a few individuals, as occurs in most places where oil is found, it has been shared out far more equitably through state intervention, ensuring, among much else, affordable childcare and long periods of paternity leave for men.

Within Norway it is recognized by many that the real secret of its success is not its oil wealth but the high proportion of women working who are paid very similar salaries and wages to men. These women are thus paying high taxes and possibly also helping to deflate incomes at the top. In many professions, when women are first allowed access, wages tend then not to rise greatly. It may be possible that greater gender equality in Norway, extending right up to the top of society, and within other Scandinavian countries, has helped to prevent top salaries rising as much as elsewhere in the rich world.

I did not include Norway in the main graph of income inequality shown earlier in this guide because in the source used here the top one per cent Norwegian income share was reported to have halved in just one year (2005-2006) which is hard to believe possible. It

Where equality can be found

may have been unduly inflated before and fell because the then government announced (in good time before it was introduced) that a new tax on *aksjeutbytter* (share income) was coming. In the following year there was a fire-sale and capital was taken offshore, where interest 'earned' on it appears to have dropped out of the top one per cent income bracket, to be brought back in later in other, less heavily taxed, ways. There is tax dodging, it seems, even in the most equitable of countries.[7]

The latest share for Norway's richest percentile is now usually reported to be about eight per cent, with the lowest ever recorded being four per cent in 1989.

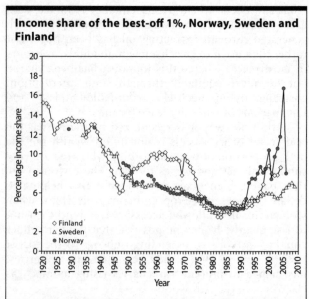

Income share of the best-off 1%, Norway, Sweden and Finland

◇ Finland
△ Sweden
● Norway

Year

Note: In Sweden the estimates exclude incomes from capital gains. In Finland the estimates are based on tax data up to 1992; but from 1993 they have been extended forwards following the rate of change of the top 1% income share based on survey data. See main text for notes on Norway.

Source: The World Top Incomes Database.

The Norwegian data has been included in the graph opposite, but it is perhaps the long-term Swedish and Finnish data which are worth concentrating on most, rather than Norway's recent blip. There have recently been increases in income inequality in these three countries, and very recently perhaps increases in equality again, but one of the things that has helped slow the effect of recent reversals has been the much greater sense of social cohesion that exists – particularly in Norway.

Greater cohesion is not the result of the shops in Norway being shut on Sundays, or the lack of a financial sector, but the consequence of many years of redistributive policies reaching deep into the fabric of society or, as my colleague Simon Reid-Henry (a part-time resident of Norway) puts it: 'nourishing its bones'.[8]

Deep down, Norway and the other Scandinavian societies have the firm foundation of a redistributive economy, which itself provides the basis for a more caring society. Many of those who favor these models suggest that it is care, as a political philosophy, that provides the basic capital for mending broken societies.

In recent years, newspapers began reporting that tensions were breaking out in Scandinavian countries as in-migrant populations grew and 'locals' began to resent wealth being distributed beyond the cohesive whole. If you look at the graph above, it suggests instead that that wealth was being redistributed towards a few well-established, affluent locals. Whenever that happens in the world, there is a tendency for the rich to try to divert attention away from their acquisitions towards some scapegoat – often towards immigrants.

Immigrants are often incorrectly blamed for part of the damage that is done by allowing inequalities to rise. This is done through perniciously claiming that it is immigrants who are taking the jobs, houses or school places that the hoarding of more and more wealth by the rich makes it harder to fund. The rise of rightwing extremism, even in Scandinavian countries, shows that they are not immune from such scapegoating when income inequalities rise.

Sweden is the country most often cited amongst the Scandinavian trio as exemplifying success. It has the highest secondary-education enrollment rate in the world, with 99 per cent fully completing high school. Compare that to just 91 per cent in the UK (but at least rising) and 82 per cent in the US (and not showing much sign of rising, according to the latest UNDP figures).

Only 0.1% of pupils drop out of their schooling in Sweden compared with 1.5% in the US and an unreported but possibly even higher proportion in the UK.[9] In Sweden there is one teacher for every 10.7 pupils, in the US one for every 14.3, and in the UK just one for every 20.1 (in most British state schools the ratio is nearer 1:30).

However, it is Finland that most often tops international comparisons of learning. Here, pupils do exceptionally well at school more often than anywhere else, and there is the highest level of enrollment in higher education. In addition, Finland's scientists publish more papers per citizen in international peer-reviewed journals than those in any other country. A few years ago Sweden topped that list.[10] This includes papers in journals covering physics, biology, chemistry, mathematics, clinical medicine, biomedical research, engineering, technology, and earth and space sciences. It is perhaps not surprising that the Scandinavians do so well in research given that they perform so well at school and university. Research and learning is best done under more egalitarian conditions – the process of peer review is itself egalitarian, in that you are judged by your peers as to whether the paper is good enough for publication.

It is not just greater ideas that are more often forged

in conditions of greater equality. The more mundane creation of everyday knowledge and information is also speeded up when more people's talents can be employed. Today, innovation is most frequently found in the most equitable of countries which are also affluent enough to foster it more easily. There are far more innovative companies produced per head of population in places like Finland (think Nokia) and Sweden (think IKEA).

In Norway, the most efficient producer of petroleum in the world, it was announced in May 2011 that plans were afoot to build the world's largest wind turbine.[11] It is easier to think ahead in more equitable circumstances. Meanwhile the greatest numbers of patents are registered (per head) in even more equitable Japan.

Very unequal places like Britain and the US like to fool themselves into thinking that they are still home to unusual numbers of inventors and especially to brilliantly imaginative entrepreneurs (a word of French origin), but no figures can be found to back up such claims. This is particularly evident in the recent most inequitable decades of life in the UK and US, which have been especially lacking in innovation other than in the financial services, where a great many recent innovations in repackaging debt recently turned very sour.

Ultimately it is innovation in thinking in general which is most free to evolve when greater equality is being realized. The stultifying atmosphere of feudal serfdom stifles the imagination of both serfs and rulers. In affluent inequitable countries, where education is highly stratified and where money buys the teaching which is often (misleadingly) presented as being best, those at both ends of the social scale end up less creative.

Children who attend the most expensive of private schools in the most unequal of affluent countries can usually have 'A' grades forced out of them, not just by the amounts of coaching they receive but by having to live in an environment where it is almost unthinkable not to concentrate so much on getting As. However, getting an 'A' isn't the same as learning. People from the top echelons of more equitable affluent countries, the Scandinavians and the Japanese, tend to be more aware.

Children who attend schools towards the lower end of the very wide spectrum of 'opportunity' offered in more unequal countries almost never attain an A, particularly in the lower 'sets' in those schools. The OECD counts secondary education spending as the total sum of both state and private spending. If you are reading this in a normal affluent country you may not be aware that in a few countries, such as Chile and the UK, as much as 25 per cent of total secondary education spending is spent privately on the schooling of just 7 per cent of children. You may also not be aware that in such countries many children are routinely put into low ability-groups at school so that those seen to be below average do not put off the more 'gifted and talented' (children really are given these labels in the UK!).

Where people are far freer to think and rest, where sham competition to identify talent is less encouraged, where there is no great corralling of children into classrooms of those of supposedly greater and lesser ability, a different atmosphere pervades. Youngsters are freer to play and associate with each other if they choose, rather than being forced to learn certain prescribed facts. Children can become interested in particular subjects and issues, and they can learn and think for the right reasons rather than simply to try to secure future advantage over others: to get an 'A'.

It is easy to become good at mathematics if you find mathematics interesting – and if you are introduced to it as interesting, rather than as a difficult subject in which you need to be coached to get the highest possible grade after several years of cramming.

Later in life, as adults, if your views are listened to in the workplace, you can help make where you work operate better. Within your organization, the more similar your pay is to others, the more you know your views are valued. If they say they value you but pay you only a fraction of what they pay themselves, then you know not to take their words seriously.

You can be a saint or a sucker and work hard in trying to suggest changes to your bosses under inequitable circumstances, but the more equal you are, the more autonomy you have to say and do what you think best needs to be done.

It is when people are given the greatest autonomy that they become most creative, that their imagination flows, that they choose to make something good. Music, sculpture, painting, writing, running, dancing, entertaining, enjoying – which of these things is best done under the cosh of inequality and which do we perform best when we are treated as equals?

Crime, gender equality and intervention

There is only one country in the world where just one person in every 200,000 is murdered each year, where only one person in every 30,000 is robbed each year, and where less than one in a hundred people have ever reported being a victim of assault of any kind (according to the UNDP). That country is Japan. This is the country which imprisons the least people, not because it is the most tolerant but because the lowest proportions of people in Japan carry out any action for which they might face the threat of imprisonment.

In countries where both income and wealth distributions are very equitable, where almost everyone else has roughly what you have, why would you plan to steal or rob others?

The Republic of Korea (South Korea) and Japan are

Where equality can be found

Wealthy countries ranked in order of equality

		Gender inequality index 2010 (world ranking)	Life expectancy at birth (years 2010)	Gross national income (GNI) per capita (PPP US$ 2008)	Income Gini coefficient (2000-2010)	Homicide rate per 100,000 people per year 2003-08	Population (millions 2010)
1	Denmark	2	78.7	36,404	24.7	1.4	5.5
2	Japan	12	83.2	34,692	24.9	0.5	127.0
3	Sweden	3	81.3	36,936	25.0	0.9	9.3
4	Norway	5	81.0	58,810	25.8	0.6	4.9
5	Czech Rep	27	76.9	22,678	25.8	2.0	10.4
6	Finland	8	80.1	33,872	26.9	2.5	5.3
7	Germany	7	80.2	35,308	28.3	0.8	82.1
8	Austria	19	80.4	37,056	29.1	0.5	8.4
9	Netherlands	1	80.3	40,658	30.9	1.0	16.7
10	Slovenia	17	78.8	25,857	31.2	0.5	2.0
11	Korea (Rep of)	20	79.8	29,518	31.6	2.3	48.5
12	Canada	16	81.0	38,668	32.6	1.7	33.9
13	France	11	81.6	34,341	32.7	1.4	62.6
14	Belgium	6	80.3	34,873	33.0	1.8	10.7
15	Switzerland	4	82.2	39,849	33.7	0.7	7.6
16	Ireland	29	80.3	33,078	34.3	2.0	4.6
17	Greece	23	79.7	27,580	34.3	1.1	11.2
18	Spain	14	81.3	29,661	34.7	0.9	45.3
19	Australia	18	81.9	38,692	35.2	1.2	21.5
20	Italy	9	81.4	29,619	36.0	1.2	60.1
21	UK	32	79.8	35,087	36.0	4.8	61.9
22	New Zealand	25	80.6	25,438	36.2	1.3	4.3
23	Portugal	21	79.1	22,105	38.5	1.2	10.7
24	Israel	28	81.2	27,831	39.2	2.4	7.3
25	United States	37	79.6	47,094	40.8	5.2	317.6
26	Singapore	10	80.7	48,893	42.5	0.4	4.8

Source: UNDP World Human Development Report 2010, various tables.

the only countries among the best-off 25 in the world where women are at least four per cent more likely to say that are treated with respect than men responding to the same question.[12] You might find this odd, since Japan ranks only 12th in the world on the gender inequality index, which reflects women's disadvantage in three dimensions – reproductive health, empowerment and the labor market. However, it may be that where there is greater overall equality, where incomes are more similar, and where paid employment is not put on so high a pedestal, gender gaps diminish.[13]

In more equitable South Korea, and especially in Japan, people live much longer lives than in less equitable countries with similar average incomes. It is women who have gained the greatest advantage, with some cohorts living up to eight years longer on average than the already very long-lived men of these countries. Overall, life expectancy is especially high in these countries because of how well women live.

The table opposite shows the 26 richest countries of the world (excluding tiny states with a population of less than two million), each with an income per person of at least $22,000 a year. The table shows the UNDP gender inequality index, as well as life expectancy at birth, mean national income, overall inequality in income, the murder rate and population numbers.

Some measures of social ill-being are only weakly correlated with inequality. Life expectancy is one such measure where, for example, heavy smoking increases death rates in otherwise equitable and healthy Denmark. Similarly, the physical exclusion of the poorest potential citizens from Singapore and Israel means the average life expectancy of all those permitted to remain within the official borders is artificially high. Another of the weaker but still significant correlations concerns how homicide rates tend to rise with inequality, as the graph below illustrates.

In the graph overleaf, three columns of data from the previous table are shown, but now made visible as positions and sizes so that you can see something of the relationship. Each circle in the graph is one of the 26 countries in the table, each drawn with circle area in proportion to population (the last column of the table). Each circle is positioned horizontally according to how high income inequality is in that country as measured by the Gini statistic (the sixth column of the table). The further to the right each circle is, the more inequitable are incomes in that country. The vertical

Where equality can be found

position of each circle is then determined by its annual homicide rate per 100,000 residents.

Among the sample shown above, of all rich countries, the country with the highest homicide rate in the world is the US and, according to the latest UN data, the UK ranks second. This is a very high rate for the UK and it may have been inflated somehow. Hand guns are prohibited in the UK and this reduces murders there. However, regardless of the validity of this one statistic, the overall relationship between inequality and the murder rate seems clear.

The country with the lowest murder rate in the world is Iceland, which is also perhaps the most equitable country of all, but its population is too small to be included above. Outside of rich countries, one of the lowest homicide rates is to be found in Bangladesh,

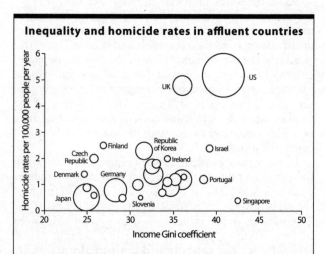

Inequality and homicide rates in affluent countries

Note: Y axis is rate by 100,000 people per year, X axis is income inequality Gini coefficient and the size of each circle is in proportion to population. Data is for 2003 to 2008. See main text for notes on the UK rate.

Source: The World Top Incomes Database, and UNDP.

which is also amongst the most equitable of very poor countries and which, most probably as a consequence of becoming more equal, has seen its infant mortality rate fall so that it now equals the world average. However on the UN gender equality index, rather like Japan, Bangladesh ranks relatively low.

Comparing Japan, a country that has kept its border intact for centuries, with Bangladesh (formed only in 1971) may appear a little foolish. Bangladesh was in crisis in the 1970s, states of emergency and martial laws were being announced, while in Japan the government was steering the economy to become the world leader in high-tech goods (in production per capita). However, it may well have been out of crises that greater equality has been secured in both Japan and Bangladesh, as compared with other similarly rich or poor nations.

It was out of defeat in the Second World War that Japan became a far more equitable nation and subsequently saw such great rises in living standards and freedoms. It was the intervention of US troops, which disbanded the aristocracy of Japan and began land reform in the late 1940s, that made that country so equal today. The US did this because it feared Japan would turn to communism if it did not, not because it was a great advocate of equality worldwide. In fact, the whole periphery of the communist bloc may have benefited from geographical proximity in the sense that this made greater equality desirable to those who feared communism.[14]

There is no determinism in history, just associations, repetitions recognized in hindsight and trends that often cease once identified. It was also out of defeat in World War Two that Singapore became, after initial anarchy, both much more equitable, then a part of Malaysia, then separate and eventually incredibly inequitable. Despite this inequality it boasts an even lower official homicide rate than Japan.

Where equality can be found

An affluent unequal population can be policed to be peaceful. Singapore has one of the largest per-capita military budgets in the Asia-Pacific region.[15] Japan has one of the lowest military budgets. Similarly, affluent countries can be at opposite extremes for income equality and military expenditure.

Similar surprising extremes can be found in very poor countries. Burundi, for example, is currently the poorest country in the world in terms of Gross National Income per capita yet it ranks highest among poor countries for gender equality. Burundi underwent its own crisis in the 1970s. In 1972, just 10 years after independence was won, a series of massacres took place there. Various Tutsi groups had been given élite positions, and partly created as an ethnic group, under Belgian colonial rule. During the 1970s some of these groups were supported by 'foreign capitalist allies'.[16]

In Burundi in 1976 a coup d'état was organized against the élite, the massacres ended, and by 1981 a new constitution had been introduced giving men and women equal rights. Despite all this, poverty rose as coffee prices fell and another coup occurred in 1987. Massacres followed again in 1989 and 1993 and another constitution was introduced in 2005. For the first time this gave the Hutu majority the chance of coming to power through voting rather than violence.

Since 1961, women in Burundi have been able to vote in elections and hold office – providing some man was not organizing a coup. In the year 2000, women held six per cent of the seats in parliament, yet by 2005 that had risen to 32 per cent, a five-fold increase in just five years. It is because of this that Burundi has the highest scores for gender equality among all 42 of the countries which the UN deems to be poorest overall.

It remains the case that, within Burundi, less than a fifth of married women have access to contraceptives, only a quarter of all people are satisfied with the standard of living, and only a third of births are attended by a skilled health worker. Yet 79 per cent of men and 83 per cent of women in Burundi say they are treated with respect.

Similarly, in Rwanda, a country with an even more bloody recent past than Burundi, over half the seats in parliament were held by women by 2008 (50.9%). Here, though, while 79 per cent of men say they are treated with respect, only 75 per cent of women claim to be, despite making up a majority of parliamentarians.

Rwanda is a much more unequal country (Gini 46.7) than similarly poor Burundi (Gini 33.3). But note how high those Gini inequality statistics are in both countries compared with those for more affluent countries. Almost all rich countries tend to be more equal than poor countries. So turn to two of the richest countries in the world. It is worth comparing the trends in inequalities in Germany and in Japan, prior to 1939 and after 1945.

One thing which is remarkable about Burundi and Rwanda is how quickly progress was made following genocide. But then the same is true of Germany following the building of concentration camps and Japan after the atomic bomb was dropped.

Most of the world is home to people who have experienced much more rapid social change than is usual in richer places, but even many wealthier countries have experienced occupation by hostile forces relatively recently. It is countries which have not suffered invasion, such as the US, Portugal, New Zealand/Aotearoa, Australia and the UK, in which old inequalities have often been easiest to defend.

The penultimate in the series of graphs that have run through this *No-Nonsense Guide* shows the share of wealth held by the richest one per cent within Japan and Germany. The last, featuring the Netherlands and Switzerland, appears towards the end of the final chapter. All four of these countries show it is possible

Where equality can be found

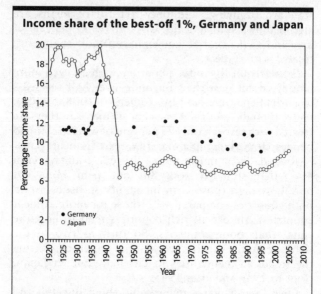

Income share of the best-off 1%, Germany and Japan

Note: In Japan the estimates exclude incomes from capital gains. In Germany the estimates are excluding capital gains apart from 1925-1938 and are only for the Federal Republic from 1960 to 1991.

Source: The World Top Incomes Database.

to hold the line. It is possible to curtail increases in inequality. It is possible to be less stupid. But it is much easier to do all these things if your parents or grandparents saw their world up-ended.

This is a book focusing on what is good about equality, so in writing it I have tried not to dwell too much on what is bad about inequality – simply listing some of the most inequitable countries in the world tends to make the point. The table early in this chapter highlights the most inequitable and equitable of rich nations. To save space, similar tables are not included for other groups of countries, but among high-human-development countries, the six most inequitable are all found in Latin America: Chile, Ecuador, Panama,

Brazil, Colombia and Belize. Among median-human-development countries three African states are included. The six most unequal are: Guatemala, Honduras, Bolivia, South Africa, Botswana and Namibia. Amongst the poorest countries, as defined by the UN Human Development Index, the most inequitable are Papua New Guinea, Lesotho, Liberia, Angola, Haiti and the Comoros islands.

Oases in apparent deserts of inequality

In June 2011, some remarkable research was reported.[17] *The Journal of the American Association for Psychological Science* announced that an upcoming issue would show that there was a psychological reason to narrow the income disparity – economic inequality makes people unhappy (see box overleaf).

Reports of this kind are increasingly frequent and very often they are produced from within some of the most unequal places on earth, in this case from within the US. It might well be because universities tend to be more collaborative places (you don't get much done in research if you don't collaborate) that these findings can still emanate so frequently from a country where so many people appear to have no great political problems with living within (and sometimes even advocating) gross inequalities.

In the US, a tenth of all adults in the labor force are currently out of work. About one in five young people are out of work, in some areas two out of five. One out of six Americans who wishes to work full-time cannot find a full-time job. There is massive hidden unemployment. One in seven Americans survive only because they are given food stamps. A similar proportion suffers from what is officially termed 'food insecurity', and is on the breadline, being very near to needing food stamps. If you live in a normal affluent country you won't know what food stamps are – look them up on the web.

Americans becoming less happy

In its press release, the American Association for Psychological Science reported that over the last 40 years, *'we've seen that people seem to be happier when there is more equality,'* according to University of Virginia psychologist Shigehiro Oishi, who (it was reported) conducted the study with Virginia colleague Selin Kesebir and Ed Diener of the University of Illinois. They found that *'Income disparity has grown a lot in the US, especially since the 1980s. With that, we've seen a marked drop in life satisfaction and happiness.'* The findings were claimed to hold true for about 60 per cent of Americans – people in the lower and moderate income brackets.

The researchers wanted to know why what they had observed had occurred. To find out, they looked at data gathered by the General Social Survey from 1972 to 2008. The survey is a poll of 1,500 to 2,000 people randomly selected from the US population every other year. The survey used to take place every year, but as a society becomes more unequal, less money tends to be spent on social-science research. The total study sample included more than 48,000 respondents and the answers they had given to that survey over the course of some 37 years.

The psychologists were interested in what appeared to explain the answers people gave to a question rating happiness on a three-point scale and to two other questions indicating the respondents' sense of how fair and trustworthy their fellow Americans were. These answers were analyzed alongside the individual's income and a measure of national income equality for each survey year.

The economist Joseph Stiglitz listed all the above statistics before he wrote in *Vanity Fair*, a magazine aimed at the rich, that *'given all this, there is ample evidence that something has blocked the vaunted 'trickling down' from the top one per cent to everyone else. All of this is having the predictable effect of creating alienation – voter turnout among those in their twenties in the last election stood at 21 per cent, comparable to the unemployment rate.'*[19] Again, it is possible to see signs that even the very affluent are beginning to realize that greater equality is in their interests.

Americans spend more on healthcare than any other people in the world in both absolute terms and as a proportion of their incomes. Given that, you may be surprised to hear that only 76 per cent of them say

The researchers concluded: *'That grim mood cannot be attributed to thinner pocketbooks during periods of greater inequality – though those pocketbooks were thinner. Rather, the gap between people's own fortunes and those of people who are better off is correlated with feelings that other people are less fair and less trustworthy, and this results in a diminished sense of well-being in general. Interestingly, the psychologists found, the inequality blues did not afflict Americans at the top.'*

The academic report concluded by suggesting that, for the richest 20 per cent, income disparity or its absence did not appear to affect their reported feelings about fairness and trust – or their own happiness – one way or the other. However, the researchers did not compare those richest Americans with affluent people in more equitable countries who – to put it bluntly – tend to be a great deal more psychologically stable, less prone to anxiety and depression and less likely to resort to drugs and alcohol to get through the day.

The positive psychological impacts of living with greater equality are one very individualist way of seeing great benefit in living in a more equal world, country, town or city. Where there is more trust of others and less destructive competition with others, people have respect for each other and so you, individually and on average, will be held in more respect and are less likely to feel so nervous, anxious and concerned. Writers such as Michael Marmot, a recent president of the British Medical Association, have linked such feelings to concerns over status in unequal settings, and the adverse effects of the hormones the human body releases into the blood stream under such conditions.[18] ■

they are satisfied with that healthcare. The table below shows which countries have the greatest and least popular satisfaction with the healthcare provided.

The Comoros islands, at the foot of the list, are among the more inequitable of the poorest countries of the world, along with Haiti and Liberia. In contrast, Austria, Switzerland and Belgium are amongst the 15 most equitable rich countries. The Netherlands and Iceland are in the top 10. But both Singapore and the UK show that it is possible to have a good public health system in an otherwise economically unequal country. It just takes a past history of greater equality and an enormous amount of defending.

But why are people not happier with their healthcare in Sweden, Norway, Finland, or Japan? Perhaps people

Where equality can be found

Adults who are satisfied with the quality of healthcare

	Rank	Country	%
Proportion most satisfied	1	Austria	93
	2	Switzerland	92
	3	Belgium	91
	4	Luxembourg	90
	5	Singapore	89
	6	Malaysia	89
	7	Netherlands	89
	8	Iceland	88
	9	United Kingdom	88
	10	Thailand	87
Proportion least satisfied	10	Nigeria	24
	9	Haiti	22
	8	Cote d'Ivoire	21
	7	Liberia	20
	6	Togo	20
	5	Sierra Leone	19
	4	Ethiopia	17
	3	Ukraine	17
	2	Senegal	16
	1	Comoros	13

Source: UN World Development Report 2010 table 10 (based on Gallup world surveys). Data are for the years 2006-2009.

in more egalitarian countries question more what might be possible. The British people might express satisfaction in their health services, but they know they need to defend them to keep them from being privatized. Britain spends one of the lowest proportions of GDP on health in Western Europe. If it fought fewer wars, it could spend more.

Equality in hopes and dreams

Many pages ago, in Chapter 2, one of the architects of greater equality in Britain was introduced. This was Richard Tawney, the brother-in-law of William Beveridge, who helped to usher in Britain's welfare state. In the 1930s, Richard and William were two of the many members of the British upper classes who came to realize that greater equality was in their interests too. With the lead being taken by working-class Labour MPs arguing against fear, their cohort made the National Health Service a reality. First printed in 1931, Richard Tawney's best-known book was simply called 'Equality'. A frequently quoted passage from it reads:

'So to criticize inequality and to desire equality is not, as is sometimes suggested, to cherish the romantic illusion that men are equal in character and intelligence. It is to hold that, while their natural endowments differ profoundly, it is the mark of a civilized society to aim at eliminating such inequalities as have their source, not in individual differences but in its own organization, and that individual differences, which are a source of social energy, are more likely to ripen and find expression if social inequalities are, as far as practical, diminished'.[20]

Richard's words were still progressive enough for a 1960s reprinting of the book, although not as progressive as his arguing against the dominant belief in racial inferiority in the 1930s. When his book is read by many people today, the statements in it often now appear romantic and paternalistic. This is hardly surprising. They were written by a man who was in his eighties at the start of the 1960s and who had died before his book was republished. He had grown up at a time when perceived differences between men and women were assumed to be inherent differences, so he only mentioned men in most of his work and in the above quotation.

Where equality can be found

Richard's views, radical in his youth, pedestrian by the time of his death, and seen as romantic now, are out of date because he had a theory that there were just a few gifted people with natural endowment who had to be plucked out of the masses and ripened for the good of the many. This idea, that men are like different varieties of fruit, of differing characters, and women are of little merit other than in their support of men, could be part of a progressive canon in one era but appear out of touch soon after. It was only progress on equality that made this possible.

Part of Richard Tawney's achievement – and that of millions of others – was to help change the world so much that they themselves now appear quaint and outdated. But progress is far from linear. Shortly after the optimism as independence was won by so many countries around the world in the 1960s, as well as great freedoms within rich countries themselves and a renewed belief in the merits of greater equality, storm clouds began to gather, and warnings were missed.

Although the Cold War 1970s were years of war, coup and massacre in many poor nations, the middle of that decade, the years 1973 to 1976, were the years of greatest wage equality in many very affluent countries, including the US and the UK. The position of women was also changing rapidly. Women would no longer play the unnamed role of purely loyal wife as did Richard's wife Janet, William Beveridge's sister. Two years after Richard died, and half a world away, Michelle was born. But the world she was born into owed a lot to people like him.

As a young girl, Michelle attended elementary school in Chicago's South Side. Her mum had been a secretary but became a housewife (or 'home-maker' in American English). Her dad was a basic-wage employee at the local water company, but his wage was enough to enable his wife not to have to work outside the home. That was the 1970s. Michelle had been born in 1964. She spent most of her childhood in a time of high and rising equality.

In Britain a few years later, a girl was born on an estate outside the gritty northern town of Scunthorpe. She was christened Samantha. Her mum didn't work outside the home either, but not because of the wages being paid to the men of Scunthorpe (even though the wages were then relatively high). Her dad was Sir Reginald Sheffield, an eighth Baronet. In the 1970s he faced high taxation. Partly to pay his bills, but also because they disliked the smell from the steel works, his family had leased the family mansion to the local council in 1963, but Samantha still got to grow up on the country estate.[21]

In April 2009, Michelle, who by now had become the wife of the president of the United States, took a detour on a visit to England. Her husband was in town to attend the G20 meeting of world leaders. Between trips to palaces and banqueting halls she popped in on an inner London school, the Elizabeth Garrett Anderson School in Islington. Unsurprisingly, perhaps, Michelle had been a little shocked by what had happened to her over the course of recent months. Perhaps it made her think anything was possible?

Michelle didn't know any of the children at the school she visited. She had never met them before. Despite this, she is reported to have choked up with emotion when addressing the girls. This is what she said:

'You too can control your own destiny, please remember that. Whether you come from a council estate or a country estate, your success will be determined by your own confidence and fortitude. It won't be easy, that's for sure, but you have everything you need. Everything you need you already have right here. We are counting on you, we are counting on every single one of you to be the best that you can be. We know you can do it, we love you, thank you so much.'[22]

Quite who had written these words for Michelle to read isn't reported, but it helps to show how the US has changed so much since Michelle was growing up, from when she herself was a schoolgirl in Chicago, and to show how Britain has also changed so much that a speech like this was greeted with adulation rather than derision and skepticism.

Two years later Michelle was back. This time she took some of the girls on a road trip (or rather they were taken on the trip and she dropped in on them, again in between banqueting and palace visiting). This time she was at the University of Oxford where she told the girls '...*this is a place for you, as well. We passionately believe that you have the talent within you, you have the drive, you have the experience to succeed here at Oxford and at universities just like it across the country and across the world.*'[23]

The only problem was that it wasn't true. It was a dream: The American Dream. The American Dream could be realized when what was hoped for was a little patch of land to build a home on 'out West'. But once the dream had escalated to having a place at a university like Oxford – there suddenly wasn't enough space. When the story came out I received a draft of a letter by Sebastian Kraemer which he sent to the newspaper that reported this story. Sebastian wrote:

'*The power of the dream is that if you believe you can make it – from inner London to Oxford, for example – there is no need to consider those who can't, to wonder where they will get jobs and homes from, or care when they are old. Mrs Obama's fervent belief that the next generation can follow her path to excellence is no match for the truth that the majority will be left behind.*'

The newspaper never printed his letter but it did later add a disclaimer to its story: '*Editor's note: in the interests of full disclosure, Guardian News Media has been involved in a community partnership with the Elizabeth Garrett Anderson School, involving charitable donation and voluntary work by members of staff.'*

And what of Samantha from Scunthorpe, the girl who did, as Michelle (in 2009) put it, 'grow up on a country estate'? Well, Samantha didn't get into Oxford University. It is unclear whether she ever applied,[24] but her future husband did, and he later became British prime minister. He was prime minster while Michelle was visiting Oxford. At the very same time as she was telling those girls they could make it, and taking tea with Samantha, he was involved in drawing up plans to privatize all English universities so that the grossly tilted playing field that had existed before was being tilted even nearer to vertical. English university education, emulating the US private finance model, was about to become the most expensive in all of Europe.

A 'celebrity-itis' has taken over in all walks of life in places like Britain and the US. The same is not found so obviously elsewhere. It screws up the thinking of well-meaning people and makes them offer vacuous platitudes. But even within these most inequitable of affluent countries, there are people telling others they have faith in them.

We'd do best to listen most to those with the greatest experience of equality, not of inequalities. We'd do well to remember that even the most affluent argued effectively for greater equality in the recent past. Those who argue for equality can include the rich and it is rarely out of envy for them that such arguments are made. A dream that we can all be more equal is realizable. The dream that we can all be rich is not.

1 JC Myers, *The Politics of Equality*, Zed, London, 2010. **2** All the figures used here come from the *UN Human Development Report 2010* or from the 2009 report if 2010 figures are missing, unless otherwise stated. Some figures for Cuba used here were missing from both those reports and so are taken from another UN source: data.un.org/CountryProfile.aspx?crName=CUBA **3** This schooling is defined by UNDP as 'the mean average number of years of education received by people ages 25 and older in their lifetime based

Where equality can be found

on education attainment levels of the population converted into years of schooling based on theoretical durations of each level of education attended'. **4** *World Guide*, 11th edition, New Internationalist, 2007. **5** en.wikipedia.org/wiki/Kerala **6** expert-eyes.org/kerala.html (more male migration of laborers to the Gulf States may be part of the reason). **7** L Gunnesdal & ME Marsdal, manifestanalyse.no **8** Personal Communication, 2011. See also nin.tl/w4T1Mj **9** *Human Development Report 2010*. The UK has an even less comprehensive system of education than the US. Of all OECD nations, possibly of all countries worldwide, only inequitable Chile spends a lower proportion on state as opposed to private education than does the UK. **10** worldmapper.org/posters/worldmapper_map205_ver5.pdf **11** nin.tl/tSM9H1 **12** *Human Development Report 2010*. **13** C Fine, *Delusions of Gender*, Icon, London, 2010. **14** Britain, the US and Canada were then free to become most unequal, as none of them was next door to a communist state except over great distances of sea or ice. **15** For details of this and of the worrying new training center for practicing fighting in urban areas see: en.wikipedia.org/wiki/Singapore_Armed_Forces **16** As the *World Guide 11th edition*, op cit, anonymously describes them. **17** nin.tl/vGzpwL **18** M Marmot, *Status Syndrome*, Bloomsbury, London, 2004. **19** JE Stiglitz, 'Of the 1%, by the 1%, for the 1%', *Vanity Fair*, May 2011. **20** On Richard Tawney, and contemporary debate on equality in Britain, see the final chapter of: A Walker, A Sinfield et al, *Fighting poverty, inequality and injustice*, Policy Press, Bristol, 2011. **21** See it at nin.tl/rCgW4u **22** news.bbc.co.uk/1/hi/7980012.stm **23** nin.tl/s6Udcv **24** A string of A grades cannot be forced out of absolutely every child, no matter how much is spent on their education. Samantha attended the same secondary school as Kate Middleton (now Duchess of Cambridge) and Frances Howell (now Frances Osborne, wife of the current Chancellor of the Exchequer, best friend of the wife of the leader of the Labour opposition in Britain, Ed Miliband). Frances met Ed's future wife at Cambridge. Ed took the same degree at Oxford as Samantha's future husband. It's a cosy little world at the top of British society. It's safe to say their school wasn't the local comprehensive.

6 How we win greater equality

Greater equality is in the interests of all – including that of the market. One bold step towards it would be to offer a basic income to all, independent of work. Above all, we need to dare to dream – and to be part of the solution, not the problem.

'People with advantages are loath to believe that they just happen to be people with advantages. They come readily to define themselves as inherently worthy of what they possess; they come to believe themselves "naturally" élite...'
C Wright Mills, *The Power Elite*, 1956

ONE WAY IN WHICH we can win greater equality is, very obviously, by depriving rich people of their unwarranted advantages. But it is just as important to explain to 'people with advantages' why a more equal society is in their best interests as well as those of the poor.

As the rest of this book has suggested, greater equality is in the interests of the rich as well as the poor because the rich then benefit, amongst many other things, from more social cohesion and trust – not to mention less crime and competitive stress. That is one aspect of the argument – but another is that the market, which is often seen as godlike by the rich, actually operates much more efficiently when people are more equal. It is not hard to show why – and one way of achieving greater equality is through explaining this to free-market enthusiasts.

Prisoners are one of the classic examples of more equal communities. Where people have similar resources then their choices are more likely to reflect their needs. Jason Myers gives the example of how prisoners-of-war will trade items in the boxes they receive from the Red Cross.[1] Those who dislike chocolates, he suggests, will trade chocolate for other items with people who are chocolate lovers. The same occurs with any other foodstuffs, with cigarettes, with paper, with pens. This works because the prisoners begin trading under conditions of equality, each having an identical box, as supplied by the Red Cross.

Markets begin to fail whenever some participants in the market start off with or accumulate more than others. The more inequitable the market, the less efficient it will be. A wealthy merchant can buy up food, not because he is hungry, but because he knows that if he does so the price will rise and he can sell at a greater profit.

Someone who is rich may buy a book just because it looks good on their shelves and not because they desperately wish to read it. That is inefficient. Markets are inefficient where some are rich and many others poor – which is why, throughout history, markets have been regulated to try to limit price-fixing, but also to ensure that it is near-equals, and mostly those who are well informed, who are making the choices.

For goods you hopefully only consume once, such as a school education or a triple bypass operation on your heart, or finding your first home of your own to live in, you are not a well-informed consumer. To become well informed requires market failure. You have to buy things and then regret buying them. This is fine with socks, chocolates, pens and paper but not with allocating surgeons, school-teachers, or housing in your twenties.

Some goods are better supplied by the market at some ages or to some people, but better supplied by the state at other ages or to other people.

It is sensible to rent housing when you first move out of the family home. You are not a well-informed consumer of housing at that point. You may also not be very interested in maintaining a home, in DIY, or in the gardening. The same may occur later in life when you may simply find it physically too hard to get up a ladder. In between those years, especially in more equitable countries, it is usual just to purchase a single family home (once in your life) and stay in it for several decades. This is because, by the time you are thinking of having a family, you tend to know a thing or two more, both about housing and about what you want in life, than when you were younger.

Free markets can be terribly inefficient. The greatest vacancy rates in housing (unoccupied homes) are found in the free market. As individuals, affluent people do not usually make great landlords. In addition, convincing youngsters to go into great debt to buy homes as soon as they can tends to backfire sooner rather than later.

In more inequitable countries, markets are usually at their least efficient. For instance, in Britain more people own more cars than they can drive at any one time as compared to the number of adults with young children who lack a car but usually would find life much easier with one.[2] People have been encouraged to buy more cars they cannot possibly need. That is inefficient.

Jason Myers gives another example of how greater inequality can be inefficient. Peasants in Britain lived in serfdom during the 13th century, yet they were quite equal to each other. Equality was high in general because mechanization was as that point largely absent and, although the lord of the manor might be greedy, he had to be nearby to collect a share of peasants' labor. As a result, claims on people's time were both more equitable and lower.

In total, before the Agricultural Revolution, British peasants worked some 1,620 hours a year – more during harvest, less in winter, but overall less than half the hours worked in 19th-century factories and still 20 per cent less than the time worked by Americans today. Myers concludes, as so many writing on inequality do, by quoting another egalitarian: *'Industrial capitalism, (as GA Cohen points out) seems to result in the confounding combination of more leisure goods with less leisure time.'*[1]

Gerry Cohen worked in the highly privileged All Souls College in Oxford, England; that same university Michelle Obama was telling the girls from London to aim for. Gerry was a political philosopher, but not one whose advice the élite followed. Michelle was simply reiterating what the mainstream US élite believes. Those on her side of the élite (Democrats in the US and New Labour in the UK) have been guided by political philosophers like John Rawls.

John Rawls advocated a particular kind of equality of opportunity and suggested that, if it were ensured, then we would end up living in a more equal world. Gerry Cohen explained why Rawls had been wrong: *'For Rawls, some people are, mainly as a matter of genetic and other luck, capable of producing more than others are, and it is right for them to be richer than others if the less fortunate are caused to be better off as a result.'*[3]

Cohen goes on to explain that it is fine to pay someone a little more to do an unpleasant job, or to take them out of a poverty trap, but that there is no need to have to use huge amounts of money to supposedly incentivize someone who appears to be talented.

If someone has developed a talent but chooses not to use it, there are – in fact – more than enough others, who will, if the talent is useful, apply theirs instead. The French publishing industry is a good example of this – it allows many thousands of writers into print, so many that, in the view of British and US publishers, it reduces the amount of profit to be made. Gerry Cohen explains why this is good: '...labor, like love, should, if given, be given freely' he suggests. And how can that be achieved? Well, by winning the argument for more equality, with some new ideas on basic income, with a bit of redistribution and reparation and some better dreaming. It can be amazing to discover what is possible.

Every great leap forward in human equality and freedom first required some people to dream. Gerry Cohen died in 2009, but a large part of what he dreamed of lives on in the dreams of many others.

The argument for greater equality

'To suggest that a specific economic, ethnic, regional or gendered group is inherently better at a particular activity would, of course, be loathsome, but we still have to admit that certain people (across the board) are better suited to certain tasks than others. The trick is to accept this and create a society that celebrates individual abilities but also sees the provision of needs (for everyone) as its most urgent priority. That is the best, most honest route to social justice and it replaces utopian pipe dreams with a blunt acceptance of the uneven texture of humanity.'[4]

What is this blunt acceptance of the supposed uneven texture of humanity supposed to be? What makes it so uneven? The phrase comes from the poet Adrienne Rich lamenting women being written off in the past and suggesting that among poor women are those who could, as architects, be reinventing our cities or founding colleges.[5] But are cities best reinvented by a single architect? And are the best colleges created from just one person's ideas?

At first it appears reasonable to suggest that we should search out talented individuals and ensure that their talents are best put to work for the good of all. But what if that search itself created great damage? What if the reality is not that there is some limited supply of individuals worthy of celebration, but that many people are capable of many tasks? What if there were not just a few who merit being celebrities? What if many are capable of great expertise? What if many can be trained as doctors (as in Cuba)? What if we work better in groups? And what if one of the key needs of all of us is to be recognized, valued and celebrated?

We are essentially equal because we are the same and have the same needs. We are not a collection of different species with greatly different requirements and aptitudes. For example, all human beings have remarkably similar requirements for food. When our nutritional requirements are consistently under or over met, even by a small fraction, we quickly become malnourished or obese. The physiological variations between us are far less remarkable than are our similarities. A world in which growing numbers (and remarkably similar numbers) of people are simultaneously starving, and dying from diseases of obesity, is a world in need of greater equality, not a world in need of a few individuals being identified by the universal talent show implied in that quotation above on the 'uneven texture of humanity'.

Evolutionary adaption has ensured that all people are now created equal. We all have an opposable thumb. It is not as if there are some people who have this advantage and others who lack it. We have created tools and machines more complex than any single individual can understand but we can each remember much less than a cheap modern computer. However, it is not our physical manifestation which most limits us or divides us, but our ability to co-operate with each other – and we co-operate best when we are more equal.

None of us are physiologically perfect. There was once an obsession with measuring variation in cranial size before it was realized that people with very large craniums often suffer from a physical illness that can cause poor mental health, such as Canavan and Hurler disease.[6]

We all have learning difficulties of one kind or another. It is just that not all of us understand precisely what our difficulties are. Me, I jumble up letters and find reading and writing very difficult, a condition with a name that is (cruelly) hard for me to spell. But finding something hard does not mean you cannot do it. All of us have some disabilities, and all of these are usually easier to cope with in more egalitarian environments.

Co-operating as equals is one of the essential traits of human beings, as fundamental to our survival as language and tool-making. In fact, what is language if it is not the basis for sophisticated co-operation? However, almost all of our ancestors lived in small groups where the adverse consequences of our actions on others were usually immediately apparent. We are currently adapting to coming together again geographically as a species in much larger groups. It is not surprising that we find this difficult.

Greater equality between individuals reduces inequality between social groups, too – this occurs between people as differentiated by age, by race, by religion, by country and by gender. Increases in income equalities from the 1920s onwards helped fuel 1950s independence movements, 1960s civil-rights movements, 1970s feminist movements and 1980s movements for the rights of sexual minorities. Greater access to universities was won by many even as affirmative action was again being opposed in the United States and as élitists in Britain were trying to establish new private universities (see box overleaf).

Winning the argument for greater equality is not, however, the easiest thing to do. It is easy enough to lampoon those who would make society less equal but it is much harder to suggest what sort of society you want without becoming very boring very quickly – or to have your own description lampooned in turn. The old Marxist idea that we should jointly decide what

Equality and the New College of the Humanities

In the spring of 2011 a series of academics, including the well-known geneticist Richard Dawkins, were involved in trying to set up an élitist private university in London. They were roundly ridiculed in the press. Dawkins tried to distance himself from the idea. The Conservative mayor of London, Boris Johnson, who had attended the world's most élitist school (Eton) and Oxford University, defended the proposed New College of the Humanities.

Amid a growing backlash from students and lecturers, Dawkins sought to clarify his role, saying on his website: *'This is the brainchild of AC Grayling, not me… Professor Grayling invited me to join the professoriate and give some lectures.'* He said *'the financial induce-ment was attractive'* and indicated he would use the fees to fund his charitable foundation.

London's mayor, Boris Johnson, backed Grayling's idea, saying *'it fully deserves to succeed and to be imitated'*. It prompted him, he added, to recall his own idea of founding 'Rejects' College, Oxbridge', which would be *'aimed squarely at the wrathful parents – many of them Oxbridge graduates – who simply could not understand how their own offspring could rack up three A-stars and grade 8 bassoon, and yet find themselves turned down'*.

The writer Terry Eagleton responded on the same day:

'British universities, plundered of resources by the bankers and financiers they educated, are not best served by a bunch of prima donnas jumping ship and creaming off the bright and loaded. It is as though a group of medics in a hard-pressed public hospital were to down scalpels and slink off to start a lucrative private clinic. Grayling and his friends are taking advantage of a crumbling university sys-tem to rake off money from the rich. As such, they are betraying all those academics that have been fighting the cuts for the sake of their students.

'If a system of US-type private liberal arts colleges like this one gains ground in Britain, the result will be to relegate an already impoverished state university system to second-class status. So far, British society has held the view that the education of doctors, teachers, social workers and so on is too momentous a matter to be left to the vagaries of the profit motive. This is why, though there are already one or two private universities in the country, nobody has a clue where they are. This new college, however, could be the thin end of an ugly wedge. Why should Grayling, Dawkins and their chums care about that, though, when they will be drawing down mega-salaries for what is reported to be an extremely modest amount of lecturing?'[7] ■

we need and that we should all share the hard (and possibly boring) work needed to produce it, maybe in the morning, is not hard to ridicule. That is, until you begin to see that in many ways we are halfway there already – it's just that many of us currently do the boring work in the afternoon too, but most of us, in the rich world at least, no longer do it in the evenings as well. This is because our grandparents ensured we are only employed legally for, at most, a third of the day.

If we managed to win more equality, we could all get the afternoons off too. This would be good not just for the working poor, but for all of us who would like to put the short single life we each have on earth to more use than paid labor alone allows. Almost no one laments not working harder for a wage on their deathbed. Chapter 5 began by suggesting that equality was the weekend. Why not extend your weekend?

Basic income and living wages

I had a shock recently. I was reading the work of a well known leftwing writer. I had got through all the pages in which he poured scorn on the stupidity of those who favor greater inequality, and the weakness of those who would just keep the status quo or want to change it ever so slightly. I was expecting to reach the usual long list of everything that needed changing, culminating in calls for revolution of some kind, but the list never came.

Instead he just suggested one thing – the provision of a subsistence-level basic income.

He did admit that '*If such a proposal were seriously canvassed by a major party with a serious prospect of holding office anywhere in the advanced world, the reaction of the privileged would be extravagantly ferocious.*'[8]

In Britain, where (as you know too well by now) I live, we have a basic income for pensioners. We have it for people bringing up children. We have it for people who are seriously disabled. It is just for the working-age childless population that we lack it and the author is right, the privileged in Britain are trying to dismantle what we have, and they are currently being ferocious in that. Notwithstanding this, Britain is one of the most inequitable countries in Western Europe and yet even it provides a basic income for many of its citizens.

In a later book, the same writer continued to make this single key suggestion. In 2010 he suggested that to get greater equality: *'In my view the best way to do this would be to introduce universal direct income. In other words, every resident of the country would receive, as of right, an income that met their basic needs at a relatively low but nevertheless decent level. This would serve two goals. First, it would ensure a basic level of welfare for everyone much more efficiently than existing systems of social provision ... Second, having a guaranteed basic income would greatly reduce the pressure on individuals to accept whatever job was on offer in the labor market.'*[9]

A year later, another writer, John Welshman, explained to the UK government that the single most important thing government could do for ending poverty would be to play down the emphasis on work. This was because so many in paid work remain poor.[10]

So-called social democrats pretend that what they call 'Welfare Reform' will give people a choice – but this kind of reform usually means no alternative to the particular paid work on offer. As British and German leaders Tony Blair and Gerhard Schröder wrote early on in their premierships, *'New policies to offer unemployed people jobs and training are a social democratic priority – but we also expect everyone to take up the opportunity offered.'*[8]

But what is unreasonable about this? Surely, you may be saying, everyone who is able to do so has to work? Well, if everything that people in paid work did was beneficial, that argument might make some sense, but the large majority of jobs are not obviously beneficial – especially in more affluent countries where so few now work the land. Many jobs involve trying to encourage people to buy things they do not think they want. From advertising executives spending a lifetime creating false desires to shop assistants asking 'would you like any help?', there are many jobs that simply serve to increase unnecessary consumption.

Thorstein Veblen wrote 112 years ago that most economic activity appeared to be addressed to trying to sell objects rather than to make them – let alone to teach, help or cure people.[11] He was writing before the advent of television advertising, before the internet existed and so before the web itself could become populated by advertising, both overt and covert.

Many jobs people currently do in the more inequitable nations are not needed in more equitable societies: prison guards, people guarding the doors to offices, all the paraphernalia of security. Similarly, if no-one is too lowly paid then it will no longer be economic to employ people to do menial tasks such as serving coffee or cleaning somebody else's home. Much can be done by machine, or by the beneficiary themselves, or by not owning property that is bigger than you need. The list of jobs that we could do without and the better things we could be doing with our time (other than being paid to work) would be very long indeed.

Basic income is also often called citizens' income. Like land value tax, along with many other progressive proposals, it can attract enormous scorn, especially for those trying to present the technicalities. It is important not to underestimate the intimidation that keeps good ideas on greater equality in an apologetic shade. Greater equality can scare people, especially when you are suggesting paying for people to do 'nothing at all for their handout'. But these same fears were raised when maternity pay was first introduced ('people will have to do nothing but get pregnant'), child benefit, pensions, and so on.

Criticism of egalitarian ideas such as basic income also often comes from the traditional Left. One anonymous person, critiquing some of Gerry Cohen's suggestions, sees it like this. '*Socialists operate within a different frame of reference, using different principles which transcend present-day society. Socialism will undoubtedly be a more materially equal society, but that is not the objective. Common ownership of the means of life will be a social relationship of equality between all people. This establishes a classless society. That is the socialist objective and not a 'fairer' capitalism...*'[12]

When it is suggested that people might be able to live more equitable lives, for example following the introduction of better basic income, detractors often suggest that this isn't real utopia, or 'socialism' as the version of utopia being described in the quotation above would have it. But one person's utopia can be another's nightmare. What does '*Common ownership of the means of life*' in the above quotation really mean?

Great inequalities have also often been perpetuated under regimes which have described themselves as socialist, just as so-called 'free market' states often contain some of the least free markets and so-called anarchists, meant to oppose over-arching forms of regulation, are often found protesting against firms that fail to pay their taxes. The political labels of old are often not especially useful.

Socialism means so many different things to so many different people that I am not going to venture a definition here; all I'll say is that the word is often used to describe a world of great equality but also of spartan living and state surveillance. In similar ways, monasteries, kibbutzim or barracks, all unusual places of high levels of internal equality, are often put forward as dystopian versions of Thomas More's most famous Utopia, where all have to be constantly surveyed. This is superficially plausible, but actually wrong.

You don't have to experience full equality to see how living just a little more equally next year, as compared with last year, could be beneficial. Greater equality allows you to love whom you wish, to trust whom you want to trust. You can escape a little more from a society in which you must always want more money, in which you must fear strangers and in which banks dictate the terms.

A more equal society is a society with more fraternity and liberty, one in which people are freer to be different, rather than each being so similar within their very stratified groups. Under inequality, you are encouraged to blame others all the time for whatever predicament you find yourself in – especially immigrants and other 'strangers': *'The Germans blame the Poles, the Poles blame the Ukrainians, the Ukrainians blame the Kyrgyz and Uzbeks.'*[13]

To gain greater equality requires co-ordination. There are groups and networks campaigning for the introduction of basic incomes and for wider social changes which often include such universal incomes. In the past, change has occurred when it has been well organized: *'The way forward toward social equality cannot come about simply through the generation and discussion of ideas... organizations are responsible for bringing about political change...[but] organizations must be brought together around [ideas] and animated by ideas.'*[1] Ideas also occasionally profoundly change the structure of entire societies. It took only a few feminists, and perhaps the birth-control pill, to lead *'...to women-friendly changes in the American base structure after 1970'.*[4]

Basic Income is a form of affirmative action. As Lyndon B Johnson said in his inaugural address as

How we win greater equality

US president in 1965: '*You do not take a person who for years has been hobbled by chains and liberate him, bring him up to the starting line of a race and then say, "you're free to compete with all the others", and still justly believe that you have been completely fair. Thus it is not enough just to open the gates of opportunity. All our citizens must have the ability to walk through those gates.*'[14] Basic income can also be seen as a way to give people freedom of choice. It opens up many more gates than just undertaking paid work, as well as giving everyone the ability to walk through those gates.

So how does a society go about introducing a basic income where every citizen receives a single equitable amount, simply for being a citizen? You begin by recognizing that, in many cases, for many groups, such a situation already exists where you live.

Many affluent countries now have a basic income for pensioners which no pensioner need live below. Similarly, basic allowances are usually awarded to all parents of children, to people when out of work, to everyone who lives in the state of Alaska or in the north of some Scandinavian countries (as incentives to live there). The result of giving all citizens an equal share of royalties from state oil exploration licenses in Alaska is that it has risen to be among the most equitable of US states – with the poorest tenth of citizens seeing their income rise by 28 per cent since the fund began, compared with seven per cent for the richest.[15]

Once a principle is accepted for one group, it is easier to extend it more widely. Once a principle is accepted at all, starting with a very low basic income, it is then possible to increase the amount without needing to argue the point of principle again.

A basic income would stop people defrauding the benefit system both because there would be less desperate need of the money among those who are currently undertaking the fraud and, more obviously,

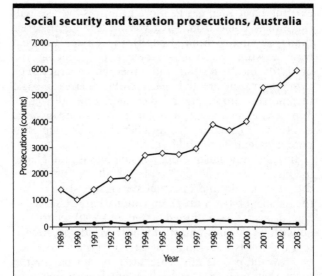

Social security and taxation prosecutions, Australia

Note: Graph first drawn by Greg Martin. The top line is the annual number of prosecutions for welfare fraud, the bottom line is prosecutions for tax fraud.

Source: D Dorling, *Injustice*, Policy Press, Bristol, 2010.

because many benefits can simply be done away with when there is no need for them under a basic income. Means-testing invites fraud and increasing poverty necessitates it.

The graph above shows how, in Australia, cases of benefit fraud have been rising in recent years. This is not just because more fraud is taking place, but also because more surveillance is taking place. The other line in the graph shows that there has been no increase in surveillance of those who do not pay all the tax they should, which often constitutes a fraud several orders of magnitude greater than even the most imaginative of fraudulent benefit claimants can achieve.

The most common question asked in response to the idea of introducing a basic income or of extending existing basic incomes to more groups is 'Where will the money come from?' Answering this is far easier than you might think. Usually the money is saved from existing inefficient schemes by reducing the need for means-testing and other bureaucracy. For example, to ensure that each child receives a basic income you simply pay all parents a child allowance and tax income, say, to pay for it. What this involves is a transfer of money from richer childless couples to poorer parents with children.

Imagine how much money would be saved if a basic income scheme one day replaced all the numerous different benefit and taxation systems existing across the whole of the European Union. How else could Europe ever have a unified system of social security to go with its free movement of labor? Mind you, money to fund a basic income scheme could also be raised by ensuring people are prosecuted for not paying the taxes they owe, as clearly does not happen much in countries like Australia.

Among many other advocates, a basic income is currently argued for by the Green Party in most countries, by Vivant in Belgium, De Groenen in The Netherlands, the Socialist Party of South Korea, the New Zealand Democratic Party, the Liberal Party of Norway, the Workers' Party of Brazil, and the New Party Nippon in Japan.[16] To be sustainable, ultimately a universal basic income would require continuous redistribution of wealth and perhaps reparation of wealth between countries.

Redistribution and reparation

The current total income bill of all US citizens is $8.25 trillion a year (see table below). If pay differentials returned to their 1970 level the total income bill would be reduced to $6.40 trillion a year. If a limit were imposed of 20:1 on what the richest could receive each year compared to the average, you would see that annual bill drop to $5.43 trillion a year – less than two-thirds of the total bill now, yet with 90 per cent of people receiving a pay rise. None of these figures are hard to calculate, so why are they so rarely discussed?

Some of the money saved by this move towards greater equality could be used to fund a US basic income scheme. Other parts of the savings could be used to establish a better (more universal) health service, to pay off some of the deficit and perhaps also to mitigate some of the inequities the US has helped to build up worldwide.

All the figures required to calculate the US wage bill are shown in the table below. In short, the richest 0.1%

Income inequality in the US, change since 1970 and what a 20:1 limit would reduce the incomes further by in comparison

Income level	Number of people	Current average income	Overall change 1970-2008 % and graph of annual change		Annual salary in 1970 (in 2008 $'s)	Salary with 20:1 limit (in 2008 $'s)
Top 0.1%	152,000	$5.6 million	385%		$1.15 million	$631,000
Top 0.1 - 0.5%	610,000	$878,139	141%		$364,000	$199,000
Top 0.5 - 1%	762,000	$443,102	90%		$233,000	$127,000
Top 1-5%	6.0 million	$211,476	59%		$133,000	$72,000
Top 5-10%	7.6 million	$127,184	38%		$92,000	$50,000
Bottom 90%	137.2 million	$31,244	-1%		$31,560	$31,560

Note: Final two columns calculated for this book given the information in the first three columns.

Sources: P Whoriskey, 'With executive pay, rich pull away from the rest of America', *Washington Post*, 19 Jun 2011.
Which in turn used The Top Incomes Database and reports by Jon Bakija, Williams College; Adam Cole, US Department of Treasury; Bradley T Heim, Indiana University; Carola Frydman, MIT Sloan School of Management and NBER; Raven E Molloy, Federal Reserve Board of Governors; Thomas Piketty, Ehess, Paris; Emmanuel Saez, UC Berkeley and NBER.

of Americans today have an average annual income of $5.6 million each. This would be reduced to $1.15 million each if income differentials were to return to 1970s levels. If American society were to become even more equitable than it was in 1970 – perhaps out of necessity following a massive and prolonged stock-market crash – and this top group were paid 'only' 20 times the average, they would have 'just' $631,000 each a year to live on.

In the US, the UK and a few other very unequal countries, it is almost taboo to suggest redistribution of income and wealth. A journalist asked Tony Blair during his 1997 campaign to become prime minister *'if there might be some small role for wealth distribution in the politics of the center left... It would have been safer to venture he regularly beat his wife'*.[17] Just two decades earlier a leader of the same political party, Labour, far from responding arrogantly and rudely as Blair did, would have given a very different answer.

It was in 1974 – at the height of income equality in Britain – that the only Labour Party manifesto to suggest including a wealth tax was written. The party won the election – but the promise was not implemented.[10] Instead, growing price inflation led to instability. It was as if the golden age contained the seeds of its own destruction.

Partly because no wealth tax was implemented, inflation was not curtailed, and unemployment was then allowed to grow. By the 1980s, people in their thirties whose parents had been poor were four times more likely than average to be poor themselves compared with only twice as likely in the 1970s.[10] If you don't keep moving forward it is very easy to move backwards.

Moving forwards in the 1970s required an idea of where you were trying to get to and the means to get to it. In places like Chile, Guatemala and Brazil elected governments were overthrown, orchestrated by US intervention. In places like Britain and the US, often the dreams presented as alternatives were simply seen as too implausible by many who might have been encouraged to dream them.

What we dream of

Here are three extremes. First, the socialist extreme. Local food production requires tractors. Tractors are made by regional manufacturing plants which assemble the parts provided by national or international factories. Local plowing requirements are calculated, orders sent to the regional manufacturers, which show in turn what requests for tractor parts they need to make to the national factories. These parts are then delivered in the knowledge that food will flow back in return. Lots of committees monitor everything – committees instead of money.[18]

A world without money is what some dream of. If this sounds like a nightmare, imagine another dream, a second extreme: where money and the free operation of the market rule everything. A tractor is then made only if it can be sold at a profit. To make a profit, the person who has the most marginal land, but can still just afford to buy a tractor, must exhaust that land until he or she goes bust. Other people must mine for the metal needed to make the tractor in the cheapest of possible conditions, often the most dangerous. More tractors will be built than are needed but also more people will go hungry.

Alternatively, imagine a third extreme, no state control at all: anarchy. Should some groups get together and wish to build tractors they might choose to. However, if some of the group wish to make their tractor work with petrol and others with clean electricity then there will be conflict, or pollution and unfair competition. No state control means no committees, but also no police and no regulation.

These three are all old arguments for what we

dream of – and all three could produce examples of extreme equality or extreme inequality. Actually, the argument that you can choose between having anarchy, or socialism, or capitalism in its purest form is silly. Nowhere do these pure, theoretical forms of society exist. You always end up with a balance, and quite how that balance is achieved determines how equitable or inequitable your society is.

As an aside, and to encourage a little optimism and realism at this point, if you do not think it is possible to see equality grow and grow, and to see the share of

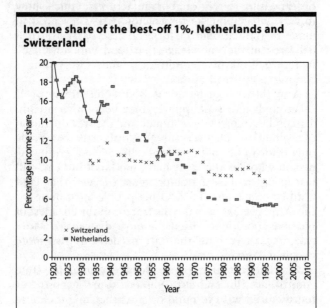

Income share of the best-off 1%, Netherlands and Switzerland

Note: In the Netherlands, up to 1946, the series is based on tabulated income tax data; between 1950 and 1975, estimates are based on tabulated data produced by the Central Bureau of Statistics; from 1977 they are estimated based on micro-data from the Income Panel Survey (IPO) and using tax and other administrative data. Swiss estimates do not include capital gains.

Source: The World Top Incomes Database.

income held by the rich continuously fall, then consider the Netherlands and Switzerland. These countries are hardly utopias. The Netherlands is the average country in the rich world by its quintile income inequality range. The Swiss are famous for their secretive banks and cuckoo clocks. But look at the graph opposite, at what people in both countries have achieved and continue to achieve when it comes to curtailing the greed of the rich.

Chapter 2 of this book was headed with the first article of the Universal Declaration of Human Rights. Let's repeat it here and ask how we as a species came to make this collective statement just six decades ago:

'All human beings are born free and equal in dignity and rights'
> Universal Declaration of Human Rights, 1948, article 1

You will almost certainly know of this. But what you may not know is who was most opposed to the introduction of just such a statement some 29 years earlier when the Covenant of the League of Nations was being drawn up. In 1919 Japan had proposed the following amendment to article 21 of that covenant: *'The equality of nations being a basic principle of the League of Nations, the High Contracting Parties agree to accord as soon as possible to all alien nationals of states, members of the League, equal and just treatment in every respect making no distinction, either in law or in fact, on account of their race or nationality.'*

On 11 April 1919 only two countries opposed the amendment, Britain and Australia. Britain was, among much else, defending its policy to make Australia a 'white only' country. A unanimous vote was needed and so the British were the ones who scuppered it. 'The defeat of the proposal influenced Japan's turn from co-operation with [the] West toward more nationalistic policies.'[19]

A friend of mine wrote to me when I was preparing this book and she said: '*I don't believe we'll get equality by voting for it, sad though that is.*' I was reminded of that when I noted that the British managed to retain inequality in international law by voting in 1919. If voting can increase and perpetuate inequalities it can decrease them too. But to make this happen we need to dream bigger dreams.

Dreams are powerful. Dreams of living under conditions of much greater equality in the future in some kind of utopia, are one of the staple means of persuading people to tolerate inequality today. From images of a heaven where there is no suffering, to being told that the rising tide will lift all boats, you are told to be patient and wait.

You are told that future technological advances will most benefit the poor and that our children will be given equal opportunities in future. Most who suggest that high inequality today has to be tolerated are rich, and they may also suggest that the future will be more equitable if we tolerate present injustices for just a little longer.

The direction in which all too many countries are currently heading belies the suggestion that the tolerance of present injustice will result in a more equitable future. This can be found in much more mundane evidence than the distribution of income and wealth.

Take New Zealand/Aotearoa, the first country in the world to introduce a welfare (social) state (in the 1930s), sometimes described after that time as being the nearest society to utopia on earth. From the late 1970s onwards, following economic turmoil, large parts of that welfare state were removed. The result was that inequalities in health between different areas of the country grew.

The graph below shows that the high level of geographical inequalities in health that came to be established across New Zealand/Aotearoa reflected the direction in which people began to migrate between different parts of the country. 'Winners' in society moved towards affluent areas and were less likely to be, to pick out one group, cigarette smokers. 'Losers' moved, in aggregate, slightly but persistently, in the opposite geographical direction.

Each dot in the graph below is a district health board of New Zealand. The white dot is especially populous Auckland. Dots drawn to the right are areas gaining male smokers over time whereas those drawn to the left are losing them. In areas drawn higher up

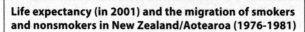

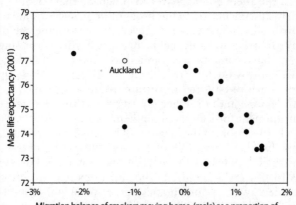

Life expectancy (in 2001) and the migration of smokers and nonsmokers in New Zealand/Aotearoa (1976-1981)

Male life expectancy (2001)

Migration balance of smokers moving home (male) as a proportion of the total population 1976-81

Note: Each circle is a District Health Board.

Source: J Pearce and D Dorling, 'The Influence of Selective Migration Patterns Amongst Smokers and Nonsmokers on Geographical Inequalities in Health', *Annals of the Association of American Geographers*, 100(2), 2010.

on the graph, male life expectancy was much higher by 2001. People become more sorted by space, health and lifestyle when economic inequalities rise.

The graph shows how movements of the population over 20 years earlier are related to inequalities today. In a society that forces people to compete more and more, the gaps between life chances by area will become ever wider. We can see it in the migratory patterns of smokers and later life expectancy by area. We can see it on the other side of the world in the way some British university students don't fight against privatization but welcome it, thinking they will all become successful consumers: '[A market in higher education] is a shared threat and one not helped by the National Union of Students' idea of becoming a consumer rights body. ("You want consumers? We'll be the consumers from hell.").'[20]

Like their counterparts in much of the US, many British students are being brought up in such a state of inequality, being examined every year from the age of five in order to rank them, that it is hardly surprising they have come to see competition and consuming as the only ways forward. Even at primary school, up to a fifth of children in Britain are now streamed for all lessons and a further quarter to a third are set by attainment for lessons in mathematics and literacy.[21]

Perpetrators of the injustice of increasing inequalities use five key tactics to offset possible public outrage at their handiwork.[22] First, they cover it up. Poverty is for 'losers' – children who fail in exams are often hidden away in poor homes and poor neighborhoods and are largely invisible to those in rich areas and in good jobs. Smokers become concentrated in poorer and poorer areas, as in New Zealand/Aotearoa. At the extreme, people with severe disabilities are often kept in institutions, excluded from the rest of society.

Second, devaluation takes place. Disadvantaged groups are stigmatized through various labels and attitudes. Prejudice is increased when there is talk of some groups as if they just can't be bothered to wake up in the morning, of the undeserving poor. This is notwithstanding the fact that the people who do least for themselves are, of course, the rich. The poor have to clean their own homes and find their own food.

Third, a reinterpretation is orchestrated. Injustice is explained away or justified through various arguments. Greed is good and necessary, for instance. Growing inequalities are presented as somehow inevitable or even desirable due to some concept such as 'globalization'.

Fourth, official channels are employed to provide a stamp of approval for inequality. For example, schooling is the premier sorting agency, while welfare systems are brought in, supposedly to help the poorest. Things seem to be fair because everything is done according to rules. The trouble is that the rules are biased.

Fifth, intimidation is used. Those who challenge inequality are at risk of being attacked. This includes trade union officials, whistleblowers, squatters, community organizers, teachers who teach about it, researchers who write about it, journalists who campaign against it. If you don't like inequality, you are somehow biased, political or unrealistic.

A comprehensive strategy to combat inequality can respond to each of these five tactics with counter-tactics that aim to increase concern and outrage over inequality. These counter-tactics fit under the categories of exposing injustice, validating targets, interpreting of practices/situations as unjust, mobilizing support and resisting intimidation.

Ultimately, however, there need to be alternatives to dream of and a reason to dream: '*Human emancipation will be a never-ending effort – to secure it where it is missing; to protect it where it is under threat; to perfect it where it is, or seems, most secure... Material growth cannot continue forever, although the growth of education, culture, music, games, information, friendship, love can.'*[23]

There are good reasons to dream. People are essentially kind and co-operative. It is just a few that want to dominate, control and be superior. Unfortunately, those few tend by definition to be much more interested in gaining power than are most of the rest of us. Nevertheless: *'Whenever an earthquake, a flood, or a drought in a far-off place leaves many victims, thousands of people in wealthier countries put their money and their efforts into providing relief. And that, too, used not to happen. Which proves that we still have the right to go on hoping for a better future!'*[24]

We can also learn from more equitable countries. Compare Britain and France. The graph in Chapter 4 showed that the French had in the last two decades resisted becoming as unequal as the British. France has much more open public debates about issues such as inequality than does Britain, and these clearly have an effect in keeping the country more equitable. In recent decades, many Anglophone social scientists have turned to translations of the work of French academics to try to understand their own countries better. It might be worth speculating why. In France, Pierre Bourdieu suggests that television presents both history and everyday events as being *'an absurd series of disasters which can be neither understood nor influenced... The journalistic evocation of the world does not serve to mobilize or politicize... The world shown by television is one that lies beyond the grasp of ordinary individuals... Linked to this is the impression that politics is for professionals...'*[25]

Pierre Bourdieu has advice for people going on television and, whenever you see someone on television or listen to the radio, it is worth asking yourself if you think his advice has been followed. Here is the advice:

'*Do I have something to say? Can I say it in these conditions? Is what I have to say worth saying here and now? In a word, what am I doing here?*' But, if you have something to say, then say it, since television holds '*a de facto monopoly on what goes into the heads of a significant part of the population and what they think*'.

What you get to hear about equality from the mainstream media in an unequal country depends almost entirely on what people say on issues like equality in the media, which is largely unconsciously self-censored because, to remain on the circuit of television invitation, pundits almost always modify their views to fit the status quo.

People who say very nasty things in private, or write them when they think only their friends are reading, try to come over as 'reasonable' on TV. Similarly, egalitarians often tend to water down their message on TV, feeling they must speak with stealth. After all, TV is the medium of celebrity culture.

You know what equality is. You have seen it if you grew up within what is now considered a normal family. You either treat your friends as equals or they are not your friends. The same with your partner, if you have one – they are not really your partner if you do not treat them as your equal.

Those who make excuses for great inequalities sometimes inconsistently suggest that there is something innate in humans that makes them desire inequality. Here is just one of many examples of a man taking his own predilections and extrapolating them to all of human history: '*Besides, a million years of natural selection shaped human nature to be ambitious to rear successful children, not to settle for contentment: people are programmed to desire, not to appreciate.*'[26]

Even in this short book it has been possible to show that evidence for such selfish and non-contemplative programming is hardly universal. Even if it were, might not many learn to change and to desire greater equality, not to be content with inequality?

If you went to a normal state school, like most people all over the world, including most that now go to university, you may at times have experienced being treated in an institution as an equal to other children. Only within the course of the last century have so many human beings experienced being treated as equal to others.

In a hospital, in a park, on the sidewalk, at a party, in any situation in which entry was not conditional on your ability to pay or denied you because of the color of your skin, your sex, religion or caste: at all these points in life you have felt what equality can be. And you should feel it especially strongly at the weekend.

Ask why next year we cannot be a little more equal than this year. Ask why the barriers between us have to rise. Ask what is being organized to avoid things getting worse and to stop a rich few taking more and more. And keep on asking – it doesn't matter how quietly, or how infrequently.

If you are questioning why we need be so unequal, you are part of the solution. If you see others as being like you, then you are part of the solution. If you are decent, and want to treat others decently, you are part of the solution.

Nobody should seek to be part of the problem.

1 JC Myers, *The Politics of Equality*, Zed, London, 2010. 2 D Dorling, *So You Think You Know About Britain*, Constable, London, 2011. 3 GA Cohen, *Rescuing Justice and Equality*, Cambridge, Massachusetts, Harvard University Press, 2008. 4 J Wright, 'More equal than others', *Geographical Magazine*, July 2010. 5 A Rich, *Blood, Bread and Poetry*, WW Norton, 1986. 6 There are other illnesses associated with large crania which are not associated with poor cognitive functioning, such as Morquio syndrome, see: nin.tl/u7oVNg 7 See nin.tl/vjkXNs and nin.tl/sIClTF 8 A Callinicos, *Equality*, Polity, Cambridge, 2007. 9 A Callinicos, *Bonfire of Illusions*, Polity, Cambridge, 2010. 10 B Knight, *A minority view: What Beatrice Webb would say now*, Alliance Publishing Trust, London, 2011. 11 PA Baran and PM Sweezy, *Monopoly Capital*, Monthly Review Press, New York, 1966. 12 LEW (anonymous reviewer), worldsocial-

ism.org Jun 2011, nin.tl/rXQ4wD **13** Z Bauman, *Collateral Damage*, Polity, Cambridge, 2011. **14** Cited in R Bell, 'Race and poverty: is affirmative action the answer?' in B Knight, op cit. **15** S Goldsmith, 'The Alaska Permanent Fund Dividend: An experiment in wealth distribution', paper presented at 9th International Congress of the Basic Income European Network, 12-14 Sep 2002. **16** en.wikipedia.org/wiki/Basic_income_guarantee **17** P Stephens, *Financial Times*, 9 Apr 1997, cited in Callinicos, 2007, op cit. **18** worldsocialism. org/spgb/pdf/saapa.pdf **19** Margaret MacMillan, *Paris 1919*, Random House, 2003, cited in en.wikipedia.org/wiki/Paris_Peace_Conference,_1919 **20** A McGettigan, '"New providers": The creation of a market in higher education,' *Radical Philosophy* 167, May/Jun 2011. **21** Millennium cohort study results summer 2011. On setting: D Muijsa, & M Dunne (2010) 'Setting by ability – or is it?' Educational Research 52(4), 2010. **22** I am grateful to Brian Martin for these suggestions, www.bmartin.cc/ **23** S George, *Whose crisis, whose future?* Polity, Cambridge, 2010. **24** EH Gombrich, *A Little History of the World*, Yale University Press, 2008. **25** P Bourdieu, *On Television*, Polity, Cambridge, 2011. **26** M Ridley, *The Rational Optimist*, Fourth Estate, London, 2011.

Index

Index

grown rich on unequal trade (selling dear and buying cheap) and on a little relaxation of the laws of usury to allow profit to be made from lending money. As yet these riches had not totally corrupted those who received them. Lorenzo de'Medici was the wealthiest of the bankers. However, he took what appeared to be gifted artists and scholars into his household where there '...*was no seating order at table. Instead of the eldest and most respected sitting at the top of the table above the rest, it was the first to arrive who sat with Lorenzo de'Medici, even if he were no more than a young painter's apprentice. And even an ambassador, if he came last, took his place at the foot of the table.*'[10]

Leonardo da (of) Vinci was just one of those young men who came to sit at Lorenzo's table (around 1480). It is ironic that the Renaissance sparked such creativity while also creating a new form of banking, epitomized by the Medicis, which made profit by lending to others and making it permissible to receive interest on those loans.

Most religions had made such moneylending a sin prior to 1480.[14] Islam continues to do so today. However, the moneylending that began in earnest in Florence quickly spread through the mercantilism of the nearby Venetian republic and was imitated more widely. For moneylending to be imitated more widely, a new source of wealth was required. Just a dozen years after Leonardo sat at Lorenzo's table, the ship Santa Maria ran aground on the coast of Hispaniola and the wealth of the Americas became available for plunder.

It was where and when religious rules against profiteering were most weakened that the vicious mercantilism of today began. One of the places made rich by banking, trade and the exploitation of the Americas – and later Africa and the East Indies – was the Dutch Republic (a queendom today). But again, like Florence two centuries before, the Republic was a place that was more welcoming of new thinking than surrounding areas. Now remembered for the Golden Age of Dutch painting, this was also the place where it became possible for René Descartes (1596-1650) to establish a philosophy of science. He would also lament how money appeared to be taking on a life of its own and maddening the minds of people in Amsterdam.

By the 17th century, the Catholic Church, which had once promoted and protected learning, had become far more dominating. Leonardo had been taken to trial for sodomy (and acquitted). The entire republic of Venice had been excommunicated. Galileo (1564-1642), the father of modern observational astronomy, came close to being declared a heretic, and a later pope placed René Descartes' books on the prohibited index, the *Index Librorum Prohibitorum*, in 1663.

Christianity, which had become a very inegalitarian

Independent shocks and new thinking in Europe

A relationship of dependence had become established between leaders of both Catholic and Protestant churches, the hereditary aristocracy and particular interpretations of the text of the Bible. This resulted in the proclamation of the supposed divine right of kings to rule – apparently a god-endorsed inequality. In Europe, it took the natural disaster of the 1755 earthquake and tsunami of Lisbon to prompt the questioning of the authority of a god (of any religion) that could sanction such misery. Yet another period of great invention was ushered in under the greater equality that questioning authority allowed. This was freedom from religious dogma and the right to have any thoughts you like (not any amount of wealth). It came to be called the Enlightenment.

'The Enlightenment broke through "the sacred circle" whose dogma had circumscribed thinking. The Sacred Circle is a term used by Peter Gay to describe the interdependent relationship between the hereditary aristocracy, the leaders of the church and the text of the Bible. This interrelationship manifests itself as kings invoking the doctrine of the 'Divine Right of Kings' to rule. Thus church sanctioned the rule of the king and the king defended the church in return.' (From the egalitarian encyclopaedia, Wikipedia).

So, over a thousand years after natural disasters helped bring Islam into existence, the Christian countries themselves had an epiphany. For the tsunami to have had such a great impact on Lisbon, that city itself religion, was propping up despotic monarchs, a corrupt clergy, and stifling all kinds of innovation. It was within this amoral atmosphere and the added influence of new-found riches from the New American World, that modern-day capitalism was born. However, a century on, another external shock, in this case the Lisbon earthquake and tsunami, would usher in more equality (see box).

It was Enlightenment thinking that culminated in the US Declaration of Independence. It was also the Enlightenment that resulted in the efficiencies of a production line version of pin manufacture being celebrated in the works of Adam Smith. In this way both greater equality and the new human enslavement (and greater inequality) of mass factory labor came out of ideas that themselves could only have been spawned in a time when we were more equal.

---

had to have grown very rich. This had occurred over the previous two centuries as gold and silver plundered from the Americas was transported through Portugal and Spain into the rest of Europe and across to India and China.

The so-called 'discovery' of the Americas was akin to a natural disaster of epic proportions for the inhabitants of those continents, who – if they survived the new diseases brought in from the old world and then the social upheaval of, in effect, aliens arriving from what might as well have been outer space (the conquistadors) – came to suffer great inequalities, destitution and enslavement. The 'discovery' also fundamentally altered world human geography. In human geography terms it recreated Pangaea (the original landmass in which all continents were joined).

Suddenly Europe took center stage as the crossroads for trade – it became the place where the Silk Road hit the sea rather than a western peninsula of Asia. In effect, it became a continent despite not being an island. The wealth that amassed in Europe as a result of trans-Atlantic exploitation was one of the catalysts for later social change being so dramatic, but it took that 1755 environmental disaster finally to sway beliefs away from the view that god approved of inequality and that he gave kings divine rights. Some 34 years after the Lisbon earthquake, revolution took place in France. Environmental and social events are always far from unrelated.[15] ∎

When we were more equal

The Enlightenment was also one of the first times when the ideas of a named woman were both taken seriously and recorded for posterity. Mary Wollstonecraft's *A Vindication of the Rights of Woman* is, in hindsight, perhaps the most significant thinking to have emerged from the Enlightenment. It was written in 1792, two years after she had written in support of the recent French Revolution, a revolt against both the monarchy and the established church. Mary Wollstonecraft was born just four years after the Lisbon earthquake and died giving birth at the age of 38. Although hardly recognized at the time, and mostly disapproved of when she was discussed, she may have been the most innovative writer of the age.

Communism, colonialism, capitalism

Rebellion often results from finding contemporary inequalities unacceptable, remembering times of greater equality and from the catalyzing effects of natural or human-made disaster. Traditionally, it was the monarch who originally provided a focus for such rebellion. Once kings, queens and emperors are deposed, the next step is the establishment of republics and of greater equality.

Western history marks out the creations of Greek, Venetian, Dutch, French and American republics – and, most recently, the creation of an economic union in Europe under no monarch – as moments of great human achievement. These moments are partly remembered in celebration because, following rebellion, the freedom to be more equal can be easily lost again and new tyrannies can very quickly become established in the wake of old. Shortly after celebration, revolution can result in terror, as occurred in France between the summers of 1793 and 1794 (often the terror is the work of counter-revolutionaries).

In all of human history, social inequalities rose most abruptly during the 19th century – and most clearly in